X8
I3

Christmas 1993

Richard —

HOME WATER
Near and Far

A nice thought!

Love —

Ilze

Books by William G. Tapply

Novels (in order of appearance)

DEATH AT CHARITY'S POINT
THE DUTCH BLUE ERROR
FOLLOW THE SHARKS
THE MARINE CORPSE
DEAD MEAT
A VOID IN HEARTS
THE VULGAR BOATMAN
DEAD WINTER
WORD PRIVILEGE
THE SPOTTED CATS
TIGHT LINES

Nonfiction

THOSE HOURS SPENT OUTDOORS:
REFLECTIONS ON HUNTING AND FISHING
OPENING DAY

HOME WATER
Near and Far

A FLY FISHERMAN'S EXPLORATIONS

William G. Tapply

LYONS & BURFORD, PUBLISHERS

Portions of this book appeared in *Field & Stream*. They have been revised for inclusion here: "On the Littlehorn" (originally titled "Home Waters"), January 1990; "Bank Shots," March 1990; "Why the Big Ones Get Away," July 1990; "A Death in the Family," May 1991; "Stretching the Hatch," June 1991; "The Extra Terrestrials," July 1991

Printed in the United States of America

10 9 8 7 6 5 4 3 2 1

Library of Congress Cataloging-in-Publication Data
Tapply, William G.
  Home water, near and far / Wiliam G. Tapply.
    p. cm.
  ISBN 1-55821-161-6
  1. Fly fishing. 2. Tapply, William G. 3. Fishers—United States—Biography. I. Title.
SH456.T36 1992
799.1'755—dc20   92-12541
                                                 CIP

This is for the pros

who row the extra mile, with thanks:

BARRY BECK

CATHY BECK

PETER CHENIER

MIKE HOWARD

WILLIAM "TAKU" JOHNSON

BOB LAMM

SANDY MOORE

PANCHO OF EL PESCADOR

BILL ROHRBACHER

DAVE SCHULLER

NEALE STREEKS

and

BEN TREBKEN

HOME WATER
Near and Far

The Education of a Fly Fisherman

FOR THIRTY-FIVE YEARS MY FATHER WROTE "TAP'S Tips" for *Field & Stream.* I've consulted my calculator to figure it out: Five or six tips a month for thirty-five years comes to nearly twenty-five hundred discrete bits of useful advice for outdoorsmen.

He stopped writing tips in 1985, but the magazine continues to reprint old ones every month. Occasionally the editors allow something outdated to appear (a lot has changed since 1950). This infuriates him.

For most of those thirty-five years Dad also wrote the "Sportsman's Notebook" column. Before he began his affiliation with *Field & Stream* in 1950, he edited sporting magazines—*National Sportsman, Hunting and Fishing,* and *Outdoors.* He edited *Trout* for three years. In 1939 he and Hugh Grey and Ollie Rodman started up a little newsletter called *Salt Water Sportsman,* which was produced, in those days, from Ollie's living room. Over the years Dad wrote countless articles on subjects as diverse as fox hunting and Atlantic salmon fishing—so many that he often used pen names.

He also wrote one of the earliest books on fly tying (*The Fly Tyer's Handbook*, which was published in 1949), and a manual on the care of fishing gear (*Tackle Tinkering*, in 1946) that inspired one of Ed Zern's most outrageously funny columns.

The Outdoor Writers of America named Dad Sportsman of the Year in 1973, an honor he continues to insist he didn't deserve.

My father never printed a tip that he didn't know would work or advice he didn't believe in or information he couldn't verify was true. People, naturally, tended to regard him as an expert. He didn't, though.

"Experts," he would say, "are expected to Know Things. That's a big responsibility. About all I know is that things change, and in the meantime it's fun to have opinions about them."

I always thought of Dad as an expert anyway, and I regarded his denials as a kind of perverse affectation. I admitted this to him once. He said, "Listen. It's good to take fishing seriously. But you should never take yourself seriously."

Dad did a lot of hunting and fishing, and I was the main beneficiary. I learned to tie flies at about the same time I learned to read. When I proved to him that I could make my own knots, hunt and fish in the rain without complaining, untangle my own backlashes, and, especially, be seen and not heard in the company of adults, I became his partner. He continued to take trips with his old friends—Tom Craven and Put and Dick Putnam, who never wrote a word about hunting and fishing; Gorham Cross, who wrote one quirky privately published volume on grouse shooting; and Lee Wulff and Harold Blaisdell and Ed Zern and Burt Spiller and Corey Ford and Frank Woolner and many others who wrote about hooks and bullets for a living. But now I got to go along. It was understood: I was his partner.

I earned the nickname "Harm." Dad's partners joked about keeping fragile pieces of equipment out of Harm's way.

I spent a lot of time in the back seats of station wagons and in the sterns of canoes and cartop boats. I took my fair turn at the paddle and oars. I can vouch for the benefits of a kid's knowing how to keep his mouth shut in the presence of grown-ups. I was, at least, tolerated. I learned a hulluva lot that way.

I can also vouch for the fact that my father knows more than he ever wrote about. I'm still learning things from him.

The best things I learned were not the tips he wrote, although I sometimes helped Dad test them out and sponged them all up as they came to me. I even came up with a couple of my own that he passed along to his readers.

It was the basic things—the assumptions, opinions, and values that lie at the root of outdoor sports, ideas that must be debated and cannot be verified, that have more importance and less usefulness than tips—that made their impressions as they came back to me from the front seat of the car or the other end of the canoe.

I learned mostly by misdirection. Dad was not big on giving lessons. I taught myself to fly cast and read a trout stream and tie a dry fly by watching Dad do it. Occasionally he'd say something like "This is the way I do it." Primarily, however, he let me try and err. I had vast enthusiasm for trying and a definite talent for erring. But I learned.

The skills are still pretty crude. The values remain constant. The opinions and assumptions, by their nature, continually change, which is what makes them the most interesting and useful.

These are some of the things I learned when I was a kid from Dad and his grown-up partners that never, as well as I can recall, found their way into print:

• There are three kinds of flies—wet flies, dry flies, and streamers.

• A fly rod is a tool used for casting flies. Most fly rods are made from split bamboo. Better rods are made of fiberglass.

• A fly reel is a kind of inert device. Its singular function is for storing line.

• The pattern of the fly you tie on is unimportant, although some patterns, such as Dark Edson Tigers, ought to be used because they are lucky.

• Fly fishing is the best because it's the hardest. Dry-fly fishing is best of all for the same reason.

• There's only one way to tie a dry fly. It imitates a mayfly and can be used at any time.

• There are two kinds of mayflies: gray ones and tan ones. Quill Gordons and Light Cahills imitate them. A #14 Adams will work fine in either situation.

• Real mayfly hatches are rare and wondrous events. The absence of a hatch is no reason not to fish with dry flies.

• If you fail to catch fish, blame your skill, not your fly.

• Damming rivers is an unmitigated evil. The Army Corps of Engineers are the devil's troops.

Introduction

• New England has the best fishing in the country. Maine has the best fishing in New England.

• The prettiest trout streams flow out of Vermont's Green Mountains.

• A tiny dry fly is a #16. A fine tippet is 4X. To use anything smaller is an affectation.

• A fourteen-inch trout is a large one.

• A small native trout is better than a large stocked one. Brook trout are natives.

• Everything has its season. You fish for trout in April, May, and June. Summer is for bass, fall for grouse hunting, and winter for ice fishing and fly tying and tackle tinkering.

• Killing a fish you don't intend to eat is a crime. Fish are better in rivers than in frying pans anyway.

• A good day of fishing is not measured by how many fish you catch or how big they are. Any day of fishing is a good day.

• It's better to fish alone than with someone who doesn't share your appreciation for the sport. A good partnership is rare and should be treasured. Fathers and sons make the best combination.

• Self-proclaimed experts such as writers are not to be trusted.

• Lee Wulff and Harold Blaisdell happen to be writers who really are experts. They let other people proclaim their expertise for them.

That I learned these things from my father, and adopted them for my own truths, does not mean he taught them to me. He taught me much, but passing off opinions for lore was not his style. I learned these things the way I'm still learning—by watching, listening, trying, and erring. It's taken me a long time to learn the importance of erring.

For all I know, Dad might not have believed any of this himself. But I thought he did, and I took these things for my own views on that assumption. A kid has to start somewhere.

So while I thank him for the wisdom contained in all of these views, I do not blame him for their limitations. They were, I believed, his opinions, the way he saw things thirty-five or forty years ago, although he never tried to force them on me. When you're a kid and you hang around adults a lot, you tend to absorb things, though you may not get them exactly right. Most of Dad's opinions as I interpreted them, I now realize, contained both truth and distortion. The true parts were his. The distortions were probably my own, although I have only begun to learn that recently.

When he insisted he was not an expert, that was a distortion that I recognized a long time ago, his own (and only) peculiar affectation. He was—and is still, now in his ninth decade—a more graceful fly caster and a better wingshot than I (nothing, however, to brag about). He ties perfect flies. He knows a lot. And he can do things. He's a compulsive tinkerer and experimenter. He's a perfectionist. He never printed a word that he didn't absolutely know was true.

He has always seemed like an expert to me.

Still, there's wisdom—which I hold in higher esteem than I do expertise, anyway—in his stubborn insistence that he not be regarded as an expert. His was not false modesty. Dad knew a lot about many things. But he was wise enough to know that he had a great deal more to learn. He recognized that real experts keep their focus narrow and deep. Generalists, he insisted, cannot be experts, but they have more fun, which is the point of it all.

Anyway, the wise man understands that few truths stand up for long, and that opinions, attitudes, and values are no measure of expertise (although they are an excellent measure of wisdom).

Dad insisted that humility is of more value than expertise. It is, I think, the root of wisdom. The man who takes his fishing more seriously than he does himself is willing to learn. He knows there is much to be learned, and he will, if given the opportunity, learn. The expert, who *knows* things, leaves no room for humility.

Dad's was not false modesty. He believed that if someone wants to proclaim you an expert, that's his problem. Dad always said, "Actions speak louder than words."

As for me, about all I'm willing to admit I know is that there's an awful lot I don't know. Every time I learn something new I'm reminded of this.

I was fishing Big Spring with Cathy and Barry Beck recently. It's a small gin-clear Pennsylvania limestone creek best fished from the bank on hands and knees, and it's populated with highly educated brook trout and a mix of skittish browns and rainbows. Barry spotted one of the browns, a fourteen- or fifteen-incher, feeding steadily in a platter-sized indentation against the far bank. We figured he was eating midges but might gobble a beetle imitation if it could be presented to him.

It was a short cast—twenty feet maybe, just the width of the stream. But the target area was a circle of perhaps six inches. The fly had to land with enough slack in the leader to allow it to remain there long enough for the trout to spot it and eat it before the current dragged it away. It was the kind of problem in fly fishing that I love.

It took me four or five casts to land the beetle the way I wanted to. It hit the water with enough of a plop for the fish to know it was there, but not so loud as to startle him, and it sat there, dragless, for a count of six.

The trout ignored it.

I cast to that fish for fifteen minutes. Every other cast hit the mark. Half of those were thrown with the proper slack in the leader. The trout continued to feed, neither spooked nor the least bit interested in my beetle.

"You try," I finally said to Barry.

"I can't do it any better," he said.

But he took the rod. And he did it much better. Virtually every cast was precisely on the mark.

After ten minutes he turned to me and grinned. "Another fish smarter than we are," he said.

I got two lessons in humility for the price of one that day, one from a smart fish and the other from a skilled fly caster. I consider that a good day.

A good day of fishing is a day when I learn that something I had thought to be true isn't. An even better day is when I can replace the old truth with a new one.

In the 1950s—my impressionable years—who could have predicted the advent of high-modulus graphite or 7X tippets that test out at two and a half pounds? Who could imagine tying a midge pupa on a #24 hook—or needing it to catch a large trout?

A true expert in the appropriate field might have foretold these things. A wise man cannot be blamed for having failed to. Dad is still incredulous when he hears of some of the developments that have occurred since he stopped writing and, to tell the truth, I get a kick out of telling him things that I've learned recently. Still, I know I'm less of an expert now than Dad was back then, although I have had to revise his truths to make them work better for me.

I think I'm holding my own in the humility department. Fish and fishermen keep teaching me about that. Still, I'm as good as the next guy when it comes to opinions. You don't need to be an expert to hold opinions, as long as you don't confuse them with expertise.

Here's what I currently believe to be true. They are opinions, nothing more. I'm positive they will hold up well for me—at least until I go fishing next time:

• Nymphs and emergers will catch more trout more of the time than any other kind of mayfly imitation. Fishing to a spinner fall may be the most fun of all. Wet flies, dry flies, and streamers have their places.

• The best tools for casting flies are made from high-modulus graphite. Something else even better will probably come along soon. But Tonkin cane has special loveliness, and by that definition makes the best fly rods.

• A fly reel is a fish-fighting tool. If you want to catch large fish you better have a good reel and treat it well.

• The color, size, shape, and action of a fly can make a difference. Sometimes all of them must be right. Sometimes none of them matter.

• Fly fishing is best because I like it best. That's the only reason. Fly casting takes longer to learn than other forms of casting, but in many situations it's the only way to catch fish. Dry-fly fishing is best because I like to see what's going on, although there's a lot to be said for the mystery of not seeing. Casting an imitation of what they're eating is the easiest way to catch rising trout.

• There are dozens of ways to make dry flies. The traditional design makes the poorest imitation of a natural dun, although it still works fine most of the time. A dry fly may imitate any sort of bug that floats on top of the water, including mayflies, caddis, stoneflies, terrestrials, and midges in several of their various metamorphoses. Dry flies rarely catch trout that are not feeding off the surface. They often work poorly even when the fish are rising. It's complicated and mysterious. That's why it's endlessly fascinating.

• There are countless species of mayflies. On some rivers many different species hatch at the same time. Trout usually select only one of them to eat, and then only a close imitation will catch them. An Adams is a good imitation for the *Callibaetis*. In quick water, trout might take it for anything. I keep reading that New Zealand trout think differently and will eat an Adams or a Royal Wulff if it's presented properly. I hope to find out for myself one of these days.

• Blind fishing with dry flies sometimes takes small trout in shallow riffled water. Otherwise, it's a pleasant way to kill time while waiting for a hatch.

• If you fail to catch a fish, you need to figure out whether it's your skill or your fly. In either case you might as well change flies, because you probably can't change your skill.

• Damming rivers is a mitigated blessing. Without its dam, the Bighorn would be a pretty good walleye fishery, and the Green and the Swift and the Deerfield and dozens of others would not be classy trout rivers. Dams, on the other hand, have contributed mightily to the eradication of Atlantic salmon from New England rivers.

• You can still find some decent fishing in New England, if you don't mind crowds. The best of it's in salt water.

• Many beautiful trout streams flow through the creases of Vermont's Green Mountains. Pennsylvania's Fishing Creek is prettier than any of them. For sheer beauty, though, I'll take the spring creeks of Montana's Paradise Valley.

• I can still tie a #16 fly onto 4X tippet without my glasses. That is my current working definition of something that is not tiny.

• A fourteen-inch trout is large in Massachusetts. It's barely average in Montana.

• A small native brook trout in New England is a rare and wonderful treasure. Native cutthroats and rainbows in the West grow large. Brown trout propagate freely in many rivers and might as well be considered native to those places.

• One can fish year-round. I do.

• I don't kill any fish that I don't intend to eat that day. I never eat wild trout. They're too precious to eat.

• I've had bad days of fishing, although the number of fish I caught was not the determining factor.

• It *is* better to fish alone than with someone who doesn't share your values. Good partnerships *are* rare. Fathers and sons *do* make excellent combinations, although other combinations, such as fathers and daughters, work equally well. Fishing with the wrong people is a good way to have a bad day. If you fish with the right people, it's just about impossible to have a bad day.

• Some writers can be trusted, although they rarely call themselves experts. Most guides know more than most writers. Writers who really are experts take their fishing more seriously than they do themselves and know enough to listen to guides.

- Lee Wulff was a myth.
- I fished with Harold Blaisdell. He was good. He took his fishing and his writing very seriously, and he held powerful opinions. He never claimed to be an expert.

The more serious I become about my fishing, and the more I hang around with other fishermen, the more I realize the magnitude of what I don't know and the more humble I grow about my own skills.

Not taking oneself seriously, I now know, is not an affectation. It's just common sense, something else I learned from my father.

I can't cast as well as Andy Gill, nor can I read a river like Mike Lawson. But I like to watch them. I feel it helps me improve. I don't know a fraction of what Dave Schuller knows about aquatic entomology or Bob Auger knows about stream ecology. But I know enough to listen. They *are* experts. They—and dozens of others—have not forced their expertise upon me. But I have learned from them. A bad day of fishing is the day I don't learn anything. I've had very few such days.

I know some things. They are, for the most part, personal truths, and although I'm willing to share them, I understand that they might not work for anyone else. I know the value of fresh air and clean water and healthy fish. I treasure the good companion. I have felt the satisfaction of refining a skill and perfecting a new trick, the exquisite thrills of outwitting one difficult fish and being bested by the next one. I've learned from fishing with other men. I've learned from books and magazines. I've probably learned the most from my private encounters with rivers and fish.

I know what gives me pleasure. I also know that this may change.

Fishing with my father is one pleasure that will never change.

My education continues. Dad still sometimes says to me, "Here's the way I try to do it." When he does, I watch closely. He and I enjoy exchanging opinions as much as we ever did. My mother calls our conversations "arguments," but we tell her they're "discussions." There's a big difference.

I'm still keeping my opinions open for revision. So is Dad.

ONE

FISH
HUNTING

FROM THE DAY MY FATHER FIRST ALLOWED ME TO follow him through a partridge cover, I was a hunter. By the time he let me carry my own shotgun in the woods, I found I had developed a sense for it. I knew where the birds would be found, how they would be likely to fly, and how I should approach them to create a shot for myself or my partner.

And I loved it.

I was then, and still am, a poor marksman. It's never bothered me—I'm not a killer. But I'm a pretty fair hunter.

I stalked squirrels and cottontails with my single-shot Remington .22 on October afternoons after school, and on weekends Dad and I piled into the car and headed for our grouse and woodcock covers in New Hampshire. I prowled swales for pheasants and marshes for ducks.

At other times of the year I hunted fish—stunted sunfish and horned pout and yellow perch in muddy neighborhood ponds, illegal bass in an off-limits municipal water reservoir, and gemlike little native brook trout in a secret rill a long bicycle ride from home.

Hunting—in all its forms—seemed to tap into something primeval in me, something instinctual that defies explanation. And, God knows, in this day and age we hunters find ourselves continually called upon to provide explanations—or more accurately, I'm afraid, excuses—for what gives us pleasure. José Ortega y Gasset may have the answer: "Thus the principle which inspires hunting for sport," he says in his *Meditations on Hunting*, "is that of artificially perpetuating, as a possibility for man, a situation which is archaic in the highest degree: that early state in which, already human, he still lived within the orbit of animal existence."

Hunting—which I and the philosopher agree includes

17

fishing—thus provides us with what he calls a "vacation from the human condition."

Golf and tennis just don't do it for us.

Ortega y Gasset says: "When we leave the city and go up on the mountains it is astounding how naturally and rapidly we free ourselves from the worries, temper, and ways of the real person we were, and the savage man springs anew in us. Our life seems to lose weight and the fresh and fragrant atmosphere of an adolescence circulates through it. We feel (it is usually said) submerged in Nature. But the strange thing is that, although Nature is not our native or habitual environment, when the hunt places us in it we have the impression of returning to our old homestead. The hunting ground is never something exotic that we are discovering for the first time, but on the contrary something known beforehand, where we might have always been, and the savage man who suddenly springs up in us does not present himself as an unknown, as a novelty, but as our most spontaneous, evident, and comfortable being."

Hunting and fishing seemed to me as a boy to be parts of the same enterprise. My mind worked the same way whether the quarry was fish or birds. The pleasures were identical. They lay in the analysis, the problem-solving, the stalk, and the outcome. Most of all, they lay in being outdoors, engaging the natural world, entering into nature's predatory essence, answering my genetically given human instinct to hunt (not, please note, necessarily to kill).

Strolling through the woods without a shotgun under my arm was the same as walking the margins of a body of water without a fly rod. Both gave definite but incomplete pleasure.

A successful outcome did not necessarily depend on

shooting a bird or landing a fish. Getting a shot defined a successful hunt. Marksmanship was a separate issue. Likewise, inducing a fish to strike at my fly or eat my worm was the point of fishing. The rewards of killing always seemed different and separate from hunting.

This has all changed very little for me. If I were a better wingshot I might think about it differently, although I doubt it. Killing a swiftly flying grouse in thick cover is an event too dependent on chance and too unusual ever to be the definitive purpose of partridge hunting. If I needed to kill to have fun, I'd hunt pen-raised plantation quail (which qualifies only marginally as hunting).

I do like to hook, play, and land my trout. But the rise is still the point of it, the definition of the successful stalk, and I rarely kill the fish I catch.

So I fished and hunted about equal time throughout my teens and twenties and found the transitions between the seasons barely noticeable. Most of the year found me carrying either a fly rod or a shotgun. Both weapons are designed for a similar purpose.

A good day of hunting was measured in birds flushed, not shot. Hunting and killing are not the same thing.

I usually practiced catch and release when hunting, too.

The more hunting and fishing I did, the more I refined my understanding of what fulfilled me most completely. My pleasure, I understood, derived from the qualities of my quarry, the environments where I found them, and the weapons I carried.

I discovered that I preferred following second-growth field edges along nineteenth-century stonewalls, crunching frost-softened Baldwin apples underfoot in abandoned orchards, clambering through alder thickets, preferably behind a close-working Brittany who'd rather point than eat. I liked ruffed grouse because they seemed smarter than I and practically impossible to shoot. I wanted to carry nothing but my little Parker twenty-gauge.

And I wanted to wade intimate streams where clear water flowed and native trout, more often than not, spurned my flies. I carried a fly rod lovingly crafted from Tonkin cane.

If my general need to fish and hunt feels inherent, my specific preference for trout fishing and grouse hunting is certainly acquired. Perhaps this makes me a little different from—though obviously no better than—bass fishermen or deer hunters. Our similarities clearly outweigh our differences.

We are all by nature hunters, I think, although nowadays more and more people among us vehemently deny their natures.

Lately I seem to be meeting a lot of folks who like to fish but scorn hunting. This also strikes me as unnatural. I suppose there are poets who write no prose and watercolorists who refuse to dabble in oils. But I suspect they, too, are denying their own natures.

I hunt birds and fish, mainly grouse and trout, and I put most of them back. Sometimes—rarely—I kill. But don't call me a killer. I'm a hunter.

1

Brine

I ONCE WROTE THE FOLLOWING SENTENCE IN AN early draft of a novel: "And, of course, there's no water whatsoever in Southern California."

My agent, a midwesterner who now lives in New York City, penned this marginal note onto the manuscript: "You may have heard that they *do* have a rather large ocean there."

Well, I guess they do, if you call an ocean water, and I was a bit embarrassed to need correcting by a landlubbing urban nonfisherman on the subject of water.

I have lived my entire life near coastal New England. I've swum and water-skied and lobstered and surf cast and handlined and trolled and thrown up in the Atlantic Ocean.

It just goes to show what happens when you obsess on trout rivers. I suspect that any trout fanatic crisscrossing the bone-dry streambeds of greater San Diego would agree

with me: There's no water that counts in Southern California.

But I should know better. Brine runs through my veins.

My parents dragged me along for a weekend at their
friend's summer house on Buzzard's Bay when I was about
six. My father had already noticed my interest in sunfish
and horned pout. It did not displease him. Correctly infer-
ring that I fully expected a dreadfully boring weekend in a
house full of adults, he drove me to the town wharf in Marion. He handed me a rusty old bait-casting rod, a bucket of
clams, and, God bless him, left me there. He knew I could
bait a hook and drop it down into the water all by myself.

"Tide's coming in," he told me. "I'll be back for you
when it starts going out."

It was, I recall, one of those gray misty-moisty summer
afternoons on the coast, the kind of day that inspires poetry
about fog and nowadays makes Cape Cod vacationers feel
they're getting gypped and impels them to clog Routes 28
and 6 and 6A in their quest for antique shops or funky sa-
loons or T-shirt emporiums or miniature golf courses or
shopping malls.

But it was peaceful out there on the end of the wharf in
Marion. Gulls screeched as they perched atop the pilings
and dove, now and then, into the water. The riggings jin-
gled quietly on the sailing craft and sleek ocean-goers that
were rocking at their moorings in the harbor. Somewhere
out in the fog a bell buoy clanged dolorously.

I dangled my legs over the side of the wharf. I cracked
open clams with a rock and jammed the meat onto my hook
and dropped it into the water. It was like the worming I did
in the pond behind my house, except that the fish I der-

ricked from the salt water were unlike any fish I had caught before. I couldn't identify any of them except a two-foot eel, which was the biggest and scrappiest fish I caught that day. Those ocean fish were uglier and larger and more abundant than what lived in the muddy pond back home, and I was entranced. That potpourri of fish swarmed around the wharf on the flowing tide. They lay there waiting for a hunk of clam meat to descend, and then they ate it and I hauled them up. I caught fish continuously and returned them all—not out of any sense of conservation, for I don't believe the catch-and-release ethic was widespread in those days, especially among six-year-olds, and even if it had been, who'd think to apply it to sea robins and sculpin? I just had no use for those fish, except to catch them. Or maybe that's the logic of catch-and-release anyway.

When I realized I would run out of clams before Dad was due to come back for me, I did kill a fish, and I hacked him into hook-sized hunks with the Boy Scout knife I always carried. And I continued to catch fish. They ate the eyes and flesh and guts of their relatives, although not quite as readily as they devoured my clams. Clam meat made better bait, I concluded—my first bit of saltwater fishing lore. And a little later, when the tide turned and the fish stopped biting altogether, I came up with insight number two.

In the forty-odd years since that day, I have had very few further insights into saltwater fishing.

My mother was born and bred in Eliot, Maine, a sleepy little New England village on the Piscataqua River, which separates Maine from New Hampshire. You have to pass through Eliot to go down east (which, of course, is really north) into Maine on the turnpike, but nobody seems to notice when they do it. My mother graduated from high school (something of a rarity in Eliot in those days) and sought her fortune at nursing school in faraway Massachusetts (which virtually nobody from Eliot had ever done before). I'm glad she did. Otherwise she probably would not have met Tap Tapply, and I could have ended up with a father who didn't like fishing.

The rest of my mother's family—my grandparents and uncles and aunts and countless cousins and second cousins and great aunts and uncles—all stayed in Eliot. We visited them on weekends, my mother and sister and I, while my father chased Atlantic salmon and brook trout and black ducks and ruffed grouse elsewhere. My grandfather and all of my uncles kept lobster boats moored in the tidal harbor of the Piscataqua. In some parts of the country everybody raises a few chickens. In Eliot, Maine, in the 1940s and 1950s, everybody had a boat and a string of lobster pots. Boiled lobster and corn chowder and apple pie were staples on my grandmother's table. I grew up eating lobster the way most kids ate hot dogs. I liked lobster. No big deal.

Haulin' pots with Grampa or Uncle Wilbur or Uncle Johnny was part of the fabric of everyday life in Eliot. I thought of it as a kind of fishing. The traps were baited with week-old fish heads and lowered on their lines to the bottom of the river to be hauled in the next day, emptied of their catch, rebaited, and dropped overboard again. The men measured the lobsters from the bases of their tails to the edges of their shells between their eyes with a metal rulerlike device. They threw back the shorts and tossed the keepers into seaweed-lined bushel baskets. Some would be sold and some kept for the table. My uncles always saved a mess of crabs from their pots for my mother, who was the only one in the family with the patience to pick out crab-meat.

When my father joined us for summer weekends in Eliot, he and Uncle Wilbur (pronounced "Woober") trolled for stripers off the back of the lobster boat. In those days, forty-odd years ago, stripers were abundant along the New England coast. The men often brought back twenty- and thirty-pounders, and then we feasted on baked striped bass—still the most delicious fish I have ever eaten.

I was too young to go trolling for stripers with the men, though I longed for it. So I waited at Gramma's house for them to return, and when they pulled into the driveway I scampered to the truck to examine their catch.

Once they came back with half a dozen huge ones.

"We caught some others, too," Dad told me. "They were rolling all over the river."

But he wasn't smiling. And he didn't seem to want to tell me about it the way he usually did.

Later that evening I overheard him tell my mother what really had happened out there that day. "We hit the tide perfectly. Fish were everywhere. We couldn't keep them away from our plugs. We kept six and then started putting them back. We'd only been there a couple hours when a boat came chugging up to us. Guy said he'd found a body in the bay. He was going after the Coast Guard. We should stay with the body. So we reeled in and went over there. He was floating face down, but it was pretty obvious he'd been in the water for a while. Woober gaffed him. I nearly puked. And we stayed there with the poor bugger until the Coast Guard arrived. By then the tide had turned and the fish were gone. It could've been the greatest day ever if it hadn't been for that dead man."

In subsequent years I trolled for stripers in the Piscataqua with Dad and Uncle Woober and made the acquaintance of that magnificent fish.

Catching striped bass was wonderful sport. But we never did land what I secretly hoped for—another dead body.

Sometimes Dad and Uncle Woober and I would chug the lobster boat under the highway bridge that spanned the Piscataqua and out into the ocean. We'd stop at some place that looked to me like all the others and lower weighted handlines baited with hunks of fish down into a hundred feet of water. We were after halibut and haddock and cod and pollock.

The heavy bank sinkers would plummet the line downward into the mysterious depths, where I imagined all sorts of monster fish must live. You could feel the line slacken when the sinker finally reached bottom. Then you lifted it a foot and held on. Soon would come a little tug-tug. A quick upward jerk of the line, then hand-over-hand you'd haul in that hundred or more feet of braided cotton line.

I always brought up one of those little sharks. Uncle Woober would mutter, "Damned dogfish," and he'd start up the engine and we'd move to a different spot.

We never caught much of anything except dogfish that I recall, and Dad and Uncle Woober always proclaimed our bottom-fishing treks out into the Atlantic failures.

Personally, I loved catching dogfish.

And as a teenager I loved handlining off Cape Cod bridges on the incoming tide and hauling up eels. I cast freshwater spinning lures into the Cape's brackish rivers and ponds for white perch, and I heaved Rapalas into the surf for blues. I always knew what I was fishing for, but I lived with the hope that one day I'd find a truly monster ocean fish on the end of my line. The brine held mysteries more compelling to me than fresh water.

I never abandoned my hope for another dead body, either.

I've rocked at anchor in the exhaust fumes of Tim Mahoney's *Leprechaun* and Ben Trebken's *Amethyst* with the rest of the tuna fleet out on Stellwagen or forty miles southeast of the Vineyard. The mates cut ripe chum and gulls materialized out of nowhere to dive for it and I sparred with nausea. We put out hooks the size of the crook made by my index finger and thumb baited with a butterfish. Our rods were an inch thick at the butt. We used blown-up balloons for bobbers.

It made bobber-watching for trout in Walden Pond seem like the sport of Lilliputians. Except for the scale, however, it was identical.

My son, Mike, caught a two-hundred-pound blue shark fishing this way—not in the same league as a dead man's body, not even a giant bluefin tuna, but a worthy monster of the deep. The mate gaffed that great fish, lifted his head up to the transom, and cut him loose.

It struck me as a waste.

We never did hook up with a bluefin.

Amethyst pulled away from the dock in the dark. It was five in the morning. My three kids and I had arisen at three-thirty. They'd surprised me. They rolled out of bed without complaining.

We chugged through the graying dawn, weaving among the moored boats in the Falmouth harbor, through Vineyard Sound, past Gay Head and Noman's Land and then southeasterly toward the horizon over seas as flat as carbon paper. We slowed briefly to watch a pod of whales loll on the surface. Soon the horizon extended all around us. We pointed toward the place where the sun cracked the sky. Ben munched a donut and studied his charts and peered squinty-eyed over the sea. He seemed to be headed someplace specific. The entire ocean looked all the same to me.

After four hours we put out lines. We trolled green-and-white rubber-skirted squid lures at high speed so that they skidded and bounced in our wake from five stubby boat rods. The fish, when they came, came in legions. A rod would begin to buck, or a line would ping out of the outrigger, and then it would zing from the reel. "Don't pick it up," Ben would say. And soon another rod would throb or another line would snap off the outrigger. We could see the fish slashing at the trolled baits only thirty or forty yards off the stern.

Once we had five fish on at the same time.

They were the strongest fish I'd ever encountered, those albacore and yellowfin. They were thirty- and forty-pounders. A couple of them went sixty. They felt like sports cars on the end of our lines. Even allowing for their greater size and factoring in the sturdiness of the gear, those tuna fought like no freshwater fish I've ever encountered. You had to reel as you lowered the rod, then try to pump the rod back to vertical. It was strength against strength, and it was a fair contest.

I kept wondering if it would be possible to catch one on a fly rod.

After noontime the seas became heavy, and Ben, his mate, the three kids, and I bounced against one another on

Amethyst. We ran out of fish. Finally around three in the afternoon we reeled in and headed back.

At five in the morning, with the day ahead of us, the long boat ride into the sunrise had been an adventure. Now we had turned, again to follow the sun's descending arc to the harbor. The ride promised to be just plain long.

An hour in, the starboard engine quit. Ben cursed, sprawled on the deck, opened a hatch, and reached into the guts of the boat. Ten minutes later he announced, "Transmission's shot. We got just one engine, folks. Gonna be a long ride."

We discovered that there wasn't a single comfortable place on the entire boat to sit or lie. We had eaten breakfast at four in the morning and our lunches were gone by eleven. *Amethyst* couldn't attain enough speed to ride on top of the chop. Every swell thudded against the bow and shook our spines. We had to hold on with both hands to keep from being thrown onto the deck. Our hands were blistered and raw from playing the fish. Our shoulders and backs and legs ached. Salt spray washed over us, stinging our wounds and chilling our bones.

It was dark by the time we raised the lighthouse on Gay Head.

We got back to the cottage at midnight. I baked tuna steaks. The kids grumbled. It had been, they unanimously agreed, the worst day of their lives.

At breakfast the next morning their faces shone. "That was awesome," they said. "What an adventure! When can we go again, huh Dad?"

I met Art at the marina near the mouth of the Merrimack at six. The fog lay so heavy over the river that we couldn't distinguish the surface of the water from the air. Art shook his head. "I don't dare go out. I'll sure as hell run into something. Let's get coffee."

We had donuts and coffee at the shop by the river and stared glumly out the window. "The blues and stripers are in," Art told me. "The tide's perfect right this minute. Damn this fog."

We had refills. We gazed out the window.

"Look a little brighter to you?" said Art after a while.

"Definitely."

"Lets go back and have a look."

Now the fog hung suspended over the flat surface of the river. The boats sat immobile and ghostly in their slips. Masts rose up and disappeared. Art squinted at the river, shaking his head. Then he said, "What's that?"

"What?"

"I saw a fish roll."

"Yeah?"

"Yeah."

"Well?"

"What the hell," he said. "Let's try it."

I had come resolutely armed only with my 8-weight graphite fly rod. So while Art crept the boat toward the flats at the mouth of the river, navigating more by memory than sight, I tied a foot of plastic-coated wire to the end of my leader and knotted on a blue-and-white Deceiver. Then I clambered forward of the cabin and braced myself at the prow. I studied the unruffled surface of the river. The tide was still coming in.

I saw a boil. Then another. I pointed and Art veered. I stripped line off my reel and began to cast. A loop caught a cleat and my fly fell short. The boils continued. We seemed to be pushing them ahead of us. I lifted my line, double-hauled, got it out there, began to strip. My fly came back just under the surface, so I saw the silvery flash just before he hit. I struck him hard, felt his strength.

"Bass," I yelled.

He was about two feet long, not a keeper. I would have returned him anyway.

My first striper on a fly.

The flats off the coast of Belize shimmer in the tropical sun in shades of cobalt and ivory and turquoise. Bonefish are mirrors. They move in vast schools through foot-deep water over the sand and coral and turtle grass. Their collective motion creates what is called "nervous water." Until I learned to recognize nervous water for what it was, I found it impossible to see.

Sometimes the schools pause and mill around, noodling at the bottom with their noses so that their tails stick up and wave in the air. It's hard to be calm when there's a school of tailing bonefish within fly-casting range.

We hunted bones on the flats both wading and from the skiff, and when we found them we cast Crazy Charlies and Snapping Shrimp into their paths and scratched the flies back over the sand bottom, and sometimes the schools spooked in a great confusion of absolutely psychotic water, and sometimes they ignored our flies. And sometimes a bone picked up our fly, and when he felt the sting of the hook in his mouth he zipped across the flats a hundred yards or more, nonstop, unstoppable. No fish could possibly swim faster.

And once, off Mosquito Cay, six tarpon cruised past and one of them peeled away from the others and ate the fly I had managed, in spite of my excitement, to heave toward him. He leapt six times. He came straight out of the water, shooting up like a Poseidon missile. He arced high above the flats, hung there, rainbowed over, and crashed back. Six times, almost without pause.

"Oh, he's a beeg one," whispered Pancho.

I instinctively bowed to him each time he jumped, depriving him of taut line to fall upon. The hook held. The tarpon swam away. I palmed the reel. Maybe I slowed him down. I could not stop him.

A few times he rolled out there on the flats. "Getting air," said Pancho. "It geeves heem strength."

Forty-five minutes later, with backing still extending far into the distance beyond the tip of my rod and the great tarpon and I at a stalemate, the hook fell from his mouth.

I reeled in, collapsed onto the seat in the bow of the skiff, and looked out over the vast fields of salt flats. It seemed as if I was seeing salt water for the first time. More mysteries lay there than I had imagined. Greater mysteries, even, than floating dead men. I would, I vowed, return to Belize.

You can find trout in Massachusetts—there's virtually no natural reproduction anymore, but big carryovers swim in some of our ponds and lakes, and the Deerfield compares well to many western rivers. Largemouth bass thrive in virtually every pond and warm-water river. Shad run up the Merrimack and Connecticut and North rivers in the spring. There are landlocks and lakers in Quabbin. We have tiger muskies and northern pike on the one hand, and bluegills and perch and bullheads on the other. Those who care for that sort of thing tell me that they find wonderful carp fishing in parts of the Charles and Concord rivers.

My father and I once caught an even dozen different species of fish while anchored in one place in Fairhaven Bay on the Sudbury River.

But the Bay State cannot truthfully boast about any of this.

Bluefish. That's what we have. There's no better bluefishing anywhere than off the Massachusetts coast.

When John Hersey wrote his book, he was writing about Martha's Vineyard. Plum Island and Cape Ann, Great Point on Nantucket, the Canal and Nauset and Cape Cod Bay—all bluefish hot spots. From June through October, Massachusetts is to bluefish fanatics what Montana is to dry-fly aficionados: Mecca.

Bluefish can—and should—be taken on a fly rod.

In past years I've trolled for blues and spin-cast Rapalas and Rebels for them, and I'm ashamed to admit that I've helped load fish lockers with more dead bluefish than we could give away.

Never again.

Blues fight strongly. They attack big green-and-white or blue-and-white streamers, stripped fast. There's nothing cautious or delicate about a bluefish, and if you can find them they're not hard to catch.

It no longer makes any sense to me to go after them with lures. Nor does it make sense to keep more than what we can eat the same day. I'd rather eat carp than day-old—or, God forbid, frozen—bluefish. Anyway, now is the time—while they're still abundant—to think about preserving this fishery. We should have learned out lessons from the striper.

Finding blues is the trick. I haven't learned it yet, so I rely on Art Currier, Walter Ungermann, Mike Hintlian, and Ben Trebken, who have boats and know their waters and their tides and their bluefish sign. They can tell which frenzy of wheeling and diving gulls signifies a school of marauding blues. They can spot the oily slicks. They claim they can smell them. "Fresh melons," they tell me. I can't smell bluefish. One more good reason to quit smoking.

Some men cast flies into the surf and catch blues. I want to learn how to do that. I want to catch just one that way. I'll have my hibachi ready. I'll drag that blue up onto the moonlit beach. I'll light the coals, then fillet my fish, and I'll get him onto the grill before his dead eyes have glazed.

I'll eat him while my hands are still wet from landing him, and I hope I'll share him with the right friend.

Then I'll return to the sea and cast my fly again, and if I catch some more bluefish I'll let them go, and if I don't catch another one it won't matter.

A McCrab tied by an American and guaranteed to sink properly costs twelve dollars. George Anderson designed this clipped-deer-hair-and-elastic-band-and-lead-putty concoction. The McCrab fly has revolutionized permit fishing.

Before the McCrab, anglers caught permit mostly as a by-product of bonefishing. It happened about as often as duffers make holes in one.

Now, hunting permit from the bow of a poled skiff in prime flats off the Turneffe Islands in Belize, skilled anglers nail permit on McCrabs with the same regularity that scratch golfers make holes in one. A permit on a fly remains the supreme fly-fishing achievement.

You are fishing with William "Taku" Johnson, the top

permit guide at Turneffe Flats. It's the last week in April. The season begins in October. Taku's clients have landed three permit this season. He's tied with Pops for the lodge lead in their private permit derby. Taku wants another. The guides take their competition seriously.

"Taku" is Creole for "north wind." William Johnson doesn't know why he was given this name.

He was once stabbed in the back in a Belize City barroom. When he reached behind himself to pull out the knife, he severed the tendons on the last three fingers of his right hand. He survived both wounds, but was left with a claw for a hand, suitable only for holding a pole.

A client, a wealthy Texan, consulted with an eminent Houston hand surgeon. Two operations later, Taku now ties flies.

Guiding fishermen out of the Turneffe Flats Lodge has lifted men like Taku and Pops, Willie and Fabian and Floyd, out of the slums. They are the elite. They take great pride in their work. They hope to be assigned competent anglers.

When you fish with Taku, you find yourself fishing *for* him. Your success is his success. You don't want to screw it up.

Flats fish such as permit and bonefish survive ospreys and sharks and all the other dangers that stalk them in the clear skinny water where they live because they are paranoid to the point of psychosis and can swim one hundred yards faster than any animal can run that distance. The soft plop of a fly hitting the water's surface, the shadow of a fly line, the unnatural silhouette of a man, and they flee first and ask questions at their leisure.

Bonefish are easier to catch than permit because there are more of them.

A school of permit is a rare sight. Usually it's spotted heading in the other direction at high speed.

To catch a permit, you must do everything right, starting with seeing the fish before it sees you. Choppy water allows you to remain invisible to the fish. It also makes the fish less visible to you.

Then you must be able to cast the heavy McCrab quickly and accurately. You must let it sink, know when to strip, how to make it behave exactly like a crab. And even when you do these things precisely right, the permit will rarely eat your fly. If you do hook one, your knots must be perfect, your reel's drag properly set. And you must have luck.

You climb onto the casting deck, strip line from your reel, give Taku a look at your McCrab in the water.

"Okay," he says.

You hold the fly in your left hand. Enough line drapes from your rod tip to allow a quick roll and cast. You check the coils at your feet. You rock on the deck while Taku poles from his platform on the stern. You squint though your amber Polaroids into two feet of water. The riffled surface makes movements of the turtle grass and coral and sand on the ocean's floor. You imagine shapes, shadows. You have never seen a permit, you don't know what you're looking for, you don't know if you'll be able to see one, or if you'll recognize it if you do.

Taku has seen thousands. "Permit!" he whispers suddenly. "Eleven o'clock."

You look. You see nothing. You begin to cast. You glance back. Taku is pointing with his pole. You will your eyes to see. Nothing. Damn! You strain. Yes. A shadow, no more. Is it a fish? You cast.

"No! Bad shot, man."

You lift, cast again.

"Right!" says Taku, all urgency and exasperation now.

You pick up again, cast to the right.

"No! You had it. No, no. Bad shot."

Language barrier, some part of your mind tells you. "Right" meant "correct," not the direction.

"Leave it. Let it sink. Now. Streep!"

You see the shadow dart, you feel your line stop. You set the hook.

"Hit heem, man! Hit heem again!"

He accelerates like a Harley. The loose coils of line snap through the guides. The fly line disappears. Backing melts off your reel. It arcs far out to sea, and still the fish swims. He will not stop. Two hundred yards of twenty-pound backing, gone. All you can do is hold the rod high and let him run against the drag. Surely he will spool you.

Then he turns, runs broadside far out there, and you retrieve some backing. He puts his flat side against you, and he feels as heavy as that monster tarpon.

You remember the tarpon. You failed to land him.

"A beeg one," mutters Taku. "Fifteen pounds."

The fish angles toward you, and you reel frantically to regain line.

"Do not force heem," says Taku. "He's hooked good."

"Twenty minutes," says Andy. "He's been on twenty minutes."

Slowly you regain line. You see the green line, you reel, then the fish silvers close to the boat. "He's beat," whispers Taku. "Be careful."

He surges, taking the fly line away. But you feel it. He *is* beat. You reel, and again the connection between line and leader appears.

There is no final surge, no boatside flurry. But your line goes slack.

"He's gone," you say. There is nothing else to say.

But you have this thought, and you know it's right: To land the first permit you ever cast to would have been a monstrous injustice. You didn't deserve it. That magnificent permit didn't deserve it, either.

You understand: It's better after you've paid your dues.

You will pay your dues. You will rock in the wind for as many hours as it takes to get another shot. It may take what's left of your lifetime, and you may never hook another. But if you do, it will be just.

Blaine Moores came to fly fishing late. Like midlife religious converts, those who discover fly fishing at an L. L. Bean or Orvis school can become even more fanatical than those of us who were born with it in our blood.

But this was ridiculous.

It was a couple of days after the arrival of the new year. The snow had come, then, in typically New England fashion, had changed over to sleet, thence to rain, before stopping. And then the temperature plummeted, and the world outside lay encased in an inch of hard ice that glittered in the frigid afternoon sunshine.

I was sitting at my tying bench inventing bonefish flies and, now and then, glancing out at the frozen world and dreaming of Belize sunshine and coral flats and ghostly shadows, when the phone rang. Long distance, from Maine. Blaine wanted to go fishing.

"Doug," he said, "got two the other day. One was nearly four pounds. Right here. Right in my backyard. Dead low tide. That's when they move into the estuary. Muddlers, size eight. Sink-tip lines."

"Whoa!" I said. "What in hell are you talking about?"

I heard him blow out a long exasperated breath. "Browns. Searuns. What else? They're here."

"The Ogunquit River?"

"Well, sure. Right out my back door. I went down yester-day afternoon. They were rolling. I saw 'em. Couldn't catch a one. But you could've."

"Oh, no. You're not doing that to me. I don't know how to catch searun trout any more than you do."

"Yeah, well, you coming, or what?"

I gazed out at my ice-shrouded world. April and Belize were months and miles away. "It's January, man," I said. "When'd you have in mind?"

"Be here Tuesday, ten o'clock," he said promptly. Blaine always has precise answers for questions such as "When?" "Tide's low at eleven-twenty. Ellen'll make a vat of pea soup for afterwards."

The pea soup did it, as he knew it would.

On Tuesday at ten in the morning the red stuff in the thermometer outside Blaine's house stood about a half-inch tall. We pulled on long johns and neoprenes and strung up our 8-weights in the kitchen. Then we waddled out the back door and over the seawall to the river.

The frigid air lifted steam off the ocean, and a twenty-knot wind blew it toward us. Five hundred yards of tidal river ebbed quietly from the bridge toward the beach. Fro-zen sand crunched under our boots, and small icebergs ro-tated slowly in the eddies.

My fingers had gone numb inside my woolen gloves.

We stood on the bank, gazing down into the water. "What now?" I said.

Blaine shrugged. "I don't know. You're the expert."

"Don't keep trying to do that to me," I said.

"Well, I don't know what to do. The fish are here, some-where."

"I'd like to see one."

"It's a kick, seeing one," he said. "We can see better from the other side. Get up higher, put the sun behind us."

We waded across. The water came to our waists. It was considerably warmer than the air.

We walked slowly upriver, peering into the water. We saw no fish.

Blaine stopped at a bend and began casting to a place where the current funneled against the opposite bank. It looked like a trouty spot, but I didn't know if searun browns hung out in trouty spots.

I kept going. At the bridge, the river divided. I chose the larger of the two channels. I cast an olive wool-headed Bugger upstream and twitched it back. Every three casts I had to stop to knock the ice out of the guides. My gloved and frozen fingers fumbled for the line. I tended to lose it on the back cast and I had to watch my hands to keep them stripping.

After a while Blaine wandered up. "Anything?" he said.

"Nope."

"Chilly."

"Yup."

We cast, fumbled for our lines, and knocked ice from our guides for two hours. The tide had turned, and the river began flowing upstream, toward the bridge.

"We better cross," said Blaine. "It's a long walk around."

The water came nearly to my armpits. It warmed my body.

Steam wafted from Ellen's pea soup the way it had from the ocean. It swam with hunks of ham. I'm going back next

week. I just want to see a searun brown trout in the Ogunquit River.

I *know* there's water in Southern California. I'm just discovering that salt water counts, even for the fly fisherman.

I no longer hope to gaff a dead man. I don't think he
would put up much of a tussle, even on a fly rod. I'd rather
catch a permit.

2

On the Littlehorn

THE LITTLEHORN RIVER IS ACTUALLY A BROOK TOO
narrow and cramped for snag-free fly casting. Roads parallel most of its length, from its origin at the outlet of a
small cottage-rimmed pond, through its meanderings behind gas stations and suburban backyards, to its termina-
tion a few aimless miles later in another pond, somewhat
larger. In April, when the hatchery trucks make their de-
posits, the Littlehorn swarms with anglers who like to
cruise red-and-white spin-cast bobbers through the pools.
Flaccid eight-inch pellet-fed brook trout gobble worms and
canned corn and cheese-scented marshmallows. By mid-
May, the Littlehorn is declared fished out.

In June the rocks in the riffles begin to rise above the
sluggish currents. Perch and bluegills and an occasional
largemouth bass move into the pools. Except for the kids
from the condominium complex, who like to hunt turtles
and frogs there, nobody pays much attention to the Little-

horn after Memorial Day. Local anglers turn to bass fishing. Dedicated trout specialists migrate to Montana and
Idaho. Serious fishermen know that the Littlehorn, like
most of our eastern trout streams, is a put-and-take fishery.

Except for me. The Littlehorn runs a mile from my
house. I consider it my private trout stream, what my friend
Cliff Hauptman calls a "home run." I know its secrets. I've
caught trout from the Littlehorn in every month of the year.

My fishing log reminds me of an unusually warm Christmas morning a few years back. Between the opening-of-
the-gifts orgy and the consumption-of-the-turkey ritual, I
excused myself and climbed into my car. A three-minute
drive found me on the well-worn banks of the Littlehorn. I
took my seven-foot glass fly rod and a box of flies from the
trunk, where I always keep them, and walked a hundred
yards downstream from the bridge. I wanted to drift a
pheasant-tail nymph against the bushes across the river
from Mrs. Rogers's vegetable garden.

If you had asked me why I want to the river that day, I
probably would have told you there was something in the
air that sparked a complex pattern of subliminal memories.
It felt right. It was a morning for fishing, Christmas or not.

Well, most mornings are fishing mornings, as far as I'm
concerned.

More to the point, I *knew* I'd find a pod of fat, blood-
spotted brookies feeding in that foot-wide run, and I *knew*
that a number-sixteen pheasant-tail nymph, dead-drifted a
foot deep, would take a couple of them.

How did I know? The Littlehorn is *my* river.

I once sat on the bank during a March snow shower and
watched half a dozen trout gorge on midges. I know I could

have caught one or two of them, but I didn't try. On that particular day, it was enough for me to know.

I used to envy friends who could call fabled trout rivers their home water—Mike Lawson, who lives and works on the banks of the Henry's Fork, Sandy Moore, who knows the Frying Pan so well that he has named several of its more prominent residents (I had a run-in with Mean Joe Green one October not long ago), and Fort Smith, Montana, denizens Dave Schuller and Bill Rohrbacher, who can trace every twisting strand of the complex fabric of the Bighorn.

These men know their rivers. I know the Littlehorn.

You won't even find an anonymous blue line on a Massachusetts road map to represent the Littlehorn River. It's on the topographic map, but it's got a different name.

The Littlehorn is my name for it. I think it's apt. The Littlehorn is exactly like Montana's Bighorn. Except it's in Massachusetts. And it's smaller.

There are holes in the Littlehorn where a careless step might send water sloshing over your hip boots. You might need more than a roll cast to reach from one bank to the other where it widens and slows below the third highway bridge. Mostly, though, it's little.

The Bighorn is a hundred times bigger than the Littlehorn. Bighorn trout, for the most part, are proportionally larger and more abundant, too.

I like the Bighorn. I admire it. I find it awesome.

But I love the Littlehorn. I love it the way some fortunate men love a special woman, intimately and without reservation. I know its flaws and limitations, its quirks and moods. I courted it for a long time before it began to respond. It's not much to look at, but to me it's beautiful.

Most of my friends, who don't know the Littlehorn very well, fail to understand the attraction.

Until you take it apart, until you separate its riffles, runs, pools, and flats and study them all, until you find the rocks and the sunken logs, the eddies and current seams—until, in other words, you invest a year's worth of hours wading and casting and sitting on the bank, watching and dreaming and allowing the stream's character to seep into your unconscious mind—until you do these things, a stream like the Littlehorn won't surrender its secrets to you.

I have done all these things. I didn't do them with any expectation that my investment would be proportionally rewarded. My reasons for wooing the Littlehorn were the same reasons men climb great mountains: I continually itched to prowl moving waters, and the Littlehorn, quite simply, was there.

I suspect, however, that many nondescript little trout streams guard the same secrets as the Littlehorn. They hide frigid little springs, deep oxygenated holes, and forage-rich channels that nourish trout, places unexceptional to the casual eye. They look like lots of other parts of the river that are barren. I uncovered the Littlehorn's secrets more by accident than design.

One August, wet-wading, I had to cross the stream to unhook a weighted nymph from a submerged log. When I reached into the water, I detected a tongue of current perceptibly colder than the rest. Ten yards upstream a spring bubbled up behind a rock. It explained a reliable hot spot. The following September I caught a five-inch brook trout from that spring hole—too small for a stocker. Anther secret: The Littlehorn holds at least a few native-born trout.

Sometimes I just walk the banks, armed with my little

glass rod rigged with a number-fourteen Adams. I don't expect to make a cast. I call it fishing, but I know it's more
diversion, a quiet communion with my stream, a couple
hours away from the desk, a cleansing of the soul. My
mind, empty of everything except the sensory things, the
gurgle of water pushing around rocks, the warbling of
birds, the smells of clean water, accepts it all indiscrimi-
nately. I'm learning, but it happens subconsciously.

Other times I study the Littlehorn more analytically. It
changes constantly—by season, by water level, by time of
day, by air temperature and relative humidity and phase of
the moon. Each combination of variables causes its trout to
behave differently. I'm still trying to factor them all. I
haven't discounted solunar and astrological theories. I still
have much to learn.

When I want to learn more about Littlehorn trout, I drift
worms on small hooks and fine tippets. It's still the best way
I know for prospecting a trout stream. I have spent entire
afternoons worming a single pool, running my bait through
the currents at different depths and from different angles.
This has taught me many things, not only about the Littlehorn, but also about the trout that live there—and, by ex-
tension, about all rivers and all trout everywhere.

I have concluded that the Littlehorn is a miniature of the
Bighorn and the Frying Pan, the Henry's Fork and the Bow,
and all the others. Littlehorn trout behave the same way
that all trout behave. They want food, comfortable oxygen
and temperature levels, protection from currents, and
safety from enemies. Trout seek specific kinds of places
that provide them with these needs. Each type of water—
riffle, pool, run, and flat—fulfills these needs in its own
characteristic way. These places are essentially the same on

all rivers. The Littlehorn is the primer that taught me to read.

I have studied the literature on the subject of analyzing rivers and seducing trout. I have fished with experts, and I've had the sense to say little and watch and listen a lot. Books and experts have unquestionably made me a better fisherman.

But that's classroom learning. Haunting the Littlehorn has given me a feel for a trout stream of any size. Those countless hours have imprinted in some largely inaccessible part of my brain understandings that I cannot articulate. But stepping into a strange river triggers a response that guides my fly selection, my wading, my casts. "There," says a voice inside my head. "Behind that rock. That resembles the corner run on the Littlehorn. A big trout lives there." I am mindless. I give my instincts their head. I'm amazed at how often those instincts prove reliable.

The Littlehorn has been my private tutor. It's mine alone. I hoard its secrets. I volunteer to nobody that I fish the Littlehorn. I insult it shamelessly if I am manipulated into mentioning it, trusting it will understand my motives. "No trout in the Littlehorn," I always say.

One June evening I made an exception to my rule. I was working my leisurely way upstream, floating a small white Wulff through a series of riffles. I was catching nothing, nor did I expect to. For now, the company of the Littlehorn was enough. I expected a hatch to come off at dusk. I would arrive at the pool below the washed-out milldam at the right time.

When I rounded the bend, I found another fisherman standing knee-deep in the middle of my pool, fly casting. She wore baggy man-sized hip boots, a long-billed cap that flopped over her ears, a blond ponytail, and a pink T shirt. She alternately slapped the water with her heavy fly rod and slapped the mosquitoes on her bare arms.

She was in my river, standing in my pool.

She was about twelve years old.

I sat on a streamside rock to watch her. She cast awkwardly and grimly. But she kept at it. Soon the sun sank behind the hill. A few cream-colored mayflies fluttered over the water. Upstream of the girl I saw a swirl. Then another. Exactly where I knew they'd be.

I couldn't stand it. "How're they biting?" I called.

She jerked her head around. "Oh, gee, Mister. You scared me."

"Sorry."

"I never catch anything. It's fun anyway."

I got up and waded in beside her. "Let's see what you're using."

She stripped in a Mickey Finn streamer, big enough to frighten a northern pike, tied to a level thirty-pound leader.

"Want to catch a trout?" I said.

She grinned. She wore braces. "Some day I will," she said.

"Why not tonight?"

She shrugged. "Why not?"

I told her my name. Hers was Maryellen. She insisted on calling me Mister. I cut off her leader and replaced it with a seven-footer tapered to 3X. Then I tied on a #14 Light Cahill and dosed it with Gink. "Cast it up there," I told her, pointing with my rod tip to the place where the current widened at the head of the pool. "There are three hungry trout there."

She managed better with the tapered leader. On her third

try the Cahill landed lightly and began to bounce over the riffled water. The fly disappeared in a silvery flash. She turned to look at me. "What was that?"

"A trout," I said. "You've got to set the hook." I demonstrated. She watched me, frowning.

They were brookies, survivors of the spring hatchery deposit. And they were cooperative. Maryellen hooked the third one she rose. She derricked it onto the bank and fell upon it with both hands.

I helped her unhook it. "Want to bring it home?" I said.

"Oh, no. Let's put him back."

I helped her unhook and revive her trout. When it flicked its tail and darted into the pool, she said, "Bye-bye, fish."

Sometimes I don't mind sharing the Littlehorn.

Few stocked Littlehorn trout survive the spring onslaught of fishermen and the low, warm waters that follow. But some do. These fish—adaptable, smart, and lucky—sometimes grow large. They accomplish this by eating. They are therefore, at least theoretically, catchable.

I consider these trout mine. I grant the May spin-casters their share. The survivors belong to Maryellen and me. There aren't enough to share.

A three-day July gullywasher a few summers ago raised the water level of the Littlehorn a foot. I donned foul-weather gear and waded into the head of the pool just below the first bridge. A big old brown trout lived in that pool. I had spied him rising a month earlier in an eddy behind an overhanging bush, an impossible lie. He wouldn't venture into the main current, which was the only place I could float a fly. So on that evening in June I quit trying and watched him. He fed methodically. I judged his size by the dimensions of the snout he lifted above the water when he sucked in the dark caddisflies that got trapped in the back-water under his bush. I had seen snouts like that in western rivers. We called them "toads." When we managed to catch toads, they turned out to be sixteen, eighteen, even twenty inches long.

On this dark drizzly July day, with the water roily and rising and the bankside bushes drowning, I hoped this toad might discard some of his caution. I tied a small weighted muddler to a 4X tippet, stripped off some line, and roll-cast it into the head of the pool. I let it sink, giving it tiny twitches as it tumbled through the dark currents.

I cast rhythmically, absentmindedly. I caught a small bass, and a little later a hand-sized bluegill. Rain trickled down the back of my neck. I didn't particularly mind. I was alone on my river. The steady hum and swish of traffic passing over the bridge behind me was muffled by the heavy air. Gradually the sounds subsided completely from my consciousness.

Somewhere in that pool lived a monster trout. Only I knew about him. I imagined him finning along the current seam, emboldened by the rising water, energized by the infusion of oxygen and the dropping water temperatures, his predatory instincts sparked by the forage drifting to him.

It took him an hour to decide to strike. When he engulfed my Muddler, I glimpsed the golden flash of his broad flank beneath the stream's surface. He turned and bulled toward the brush-lined opposite bank. On 4X, I could only raise my rod tip and let the line slide through my fingers. He turned and headed downstream. He jumped once. A toad.

The sounds of traffic filtered back into my consciousness. I was standing there, in plain sight, with a large trout on the end of my line. I considered the consequences.

I snubbed the line around my finger and lowered my rod to give the fish a straight pull. I felt the leader tighten, stretch, then pop. "Bye-bye, fish," I said. Some things are more important than catching a big trout.

3

A Death in the Family

GOOSE POND NESTLES AT THE FOOT OF THE HILL,
less than a mile from home. It's a typical suburban pond,
maybe twenty-five acres, no more. The neighborhood kids
build rafts and launch them from the pond's shores. The
older ones paddle out to Boy Scout Island and camp there
in the summer. In August the blueberry bushes on the island attract cedar waxwings and cardinals. Courting
couples drift aimlessly on my pond's surface, trailing their
hands over the sides of their canoes or dangling their feet
from their rubber rafts, enjoying the sunshine and plucking
water lilies and admiring the birds. In the winter, the entire
neighborhood turns out for bonfires and ice-skating par-
ties.

It's the place where all the local kids—and some non-
goal-oriented local adults, too—go fishing. It's a perfect
spot for contemplating a red-and-white bobber.

My son Michael caught his first trout from the brook that

feeds Goose Pond on our first expedition there when he was nine. Two years later his sister, Melissa, accurately pro-claimed herself a "crappie fisherman" after her first trip to the pond with me.

It was the place I used to escape to for an hour or two of solitude on a summer's evening. Alone in my canoe with my fly rod, I found largemouths and pickerel lurking under the lily pads and against the shorelines overhung with those blueberry bushes. Sometimes I'd cast a wet fly and see how many different species of panfish I could catch while the sky darkened and swallows ticked the water's skin with their wingtips. The spat of bluegills mingled with the grumble of bullfrogs and the cooing of night birds, and I barely noticed the muffled swish of highway traffic beyond the tree line.

In those days I occasionally found myself sharing the pond with men in bass boats. A bass boat on Goose Pond always seemed as out of place to me as a Mercedes at the Soapbox Derby. Their roaring outboard motors, their depth-finders and foot-operated electric motors, their bristle of spinning rods, all of it vaguely offended me. Bass boats, I suppose, have their place. But Goose was a neigh-borhood pond, a place for canoes and inflatable rubber rafts, a place for kids, or for kids with their fathers, or just for fathers after a tough day's drudgery in the city.

Most of these high-tech craft, I learned from talking with the men who operated them, had been trailered in from out of town, occasionally even from out of state. I made it a point to talk with these aliens, amazed and amused that they had come so far to fish this little place a half-mile from where I lived. They told me tales of eight-pound bass. I never believed them. No one could have fished Goose Pond more than I, and I had never caught a bass bigger than two pounds there.

And yet they *had* come all that distance . . .

I *didn't* believe them. A two-pounder, I knew, could transform itself in the telling and retelling into an eight-pounder. Still . . .

So I tried crawling plastic worms through the deep holes. I tried live minnows and nightcrawlers and crawfish. I caught plenty of two-pounders, which was fine with me. I liked the idea of a lunker living in my pond, but I had no particular desire to catch it any more than I wanted some-one else to.

Goose Pond teemed with fish. There were the bass and the pickerel. Schools of fat one-pound crappies. White perch and yellow perch and horned pout and suckers and carp. Saucer-size bluegills that gobbled the panfish pop-pers that Michael and Melissa managed to cast from the canoe. In the springtime trout wandered into the pond from the brook that fed it. There were stories of a ten-pound brown trout taken from my pond, too.

Herons and muskrats and wood ducks lived there, and flocks of mallards and blacks and Canadas dropped in on their migrations. It's rimmed with trees and marshland, and in spite of its location in the middle of a densely pop-ulated Boston suburb, floating on Goose Pond in a canoe always gave me the illusion of being in the wilderness.

It's been a perfect place to introduce my kids to fishing.

Before that Saturday last July, I hadn't been to Goose Pond for several years. The two older kids felt they had out-grown our neighborhood pond, so when I've taken them fishing lately we've ventured farther from home. And I've discovered a couple of other ponds for my solitude where the bass really do grow larger than two pounds, and which are accessible only to float tubes.

When I asked Sarah, my younger daughter, if she wanted to go fishing that day, she grinned and said, "Sure. Where?"

"Goose Pond. We'll take the canoe."

Sarah didn't understand, and I didn't bother to explain, that this was to be a ceremonial occasion. We had dangled worms under bobbers together a few times, and I often took all the kids out on a boat with me. But this would be the first real fishing trip for just the two of us, father and daughter, and we would do it at the same place I had taken Michael when *he* was about nine, and Melissa, too, when she was that same age.

It was, of course, a father's ceremony. Nine-year-old kids aren't big on ceremonies.

There were no other cars at the sand beach. Unusual for a sparkling Saturday afternoon in early July, I thought, but I was grateful that Sarah and I would have the place to ourselves.

She insisted that she wanted to show me all she had learned about canoe-paddling at her Girl Scout camp. "Okay," I said. "We'll take turns." So I tied on a buggy panfish-size streamer and began to cast while Sarah zigged and zagged us more or less parallel to the shoreline.

And I instantly knew something was terribly wrong.

Weeds. Big shapeless hunks of gunky green crud that clung to my fly like the globs of old hair from a clogged shower drain. Ropelike weeds so thick that Sarah's paddle stuck in them. Except for a clear patch along the windward shore, the surface of the pond was blanketed with weeds so solidly that it looked as if one could walk on it.

I heard no *spat-spat* of feeding bluegills. No bullfrogs grumped along the shore.

The water was the color of pea soup.

I dropped my fly into the narrow channels and holes among the weeds. I switched to a floater. I fished hard.

I never had a strike.

Since I had last been there, Goose Pond had died.

I know that ponds, like all living organisms, do not live forever. Eutrophic ponds such as Goose—warm, shallow, rich in life-giving nutrients such as oxygen, carbon dioxide, and various compounds of nitrogen, calcium, potassium, and phosphorus—are continuously changing. They are born, they grow, they mature, they age, they die. It's a natural, dynamic process.

Weeds grow in ponds. Aquatic vegetation in normal ecological balance nurtures plankton, crustaceans, insects, and other life forms that feed fish. Weed beds provide protection for fish and frogs and turtles, dragonflies and damselflies and skaters. Water weeds, in other words, are essential for the health of a pond and all its denizens.

When the vegetation dies in the winter, it sinks to the bottom, where it rots and provides a fertile growing medium for its next generation, and so on through the years. Gradually the weed beds thicken and spread over the surface of the pond, blocking sunlight and choking off the water's oxygen supply. Vegetation around the rim of the pond marches toward the center. And each year through the cycle of growing and dying vegetation, the pond bottom rises closer to the surface and grows increasingly rich in the nutrients that feed water weeds. Eventually, the masses of rotting vegetation emit gasses in quantities that kill, rather than nurture, aquatic life. Inevitably, as sediment accumulates, the bottom reaches the surface and the pond becomes a swamp, then a marsh, then a meadow.

I knew this. But I also knew that it normally happens so slowly as to be unnoticeable from year to year.

Afterwards a local aquatic biologist explained it to me. "It's simple," he said. "Your pond has been poisoned. Oh, Goose isn't polluted, at least not in the usual sense. We tested it couple of years ago. No PCBs, no toxins to speak of. The pond is just superfertile, primarily the result of run-off of agricultural fertilizers from the cornfields along the brook that feeds it plus seepage from nearby septic systems. Nobody's fault, really. Nobody broke any law. The natural balance has been ruined, that's all. The vegetation is growing out of control. The fish can't compete with the weeds. The pond's life cycle has been accelerated. Simple as that. Nothing anybody can do about it now. It's dead."

Goose Pond, I understood, hadn't really been murdered. But it didn't die a natural death, either. It was simply another innocent victim of civilization. And my kids and I are poorer for it.

Sarah struggled bravely with the paddle, but finally she said, "I can't make it go, Daddy. There's too many weeds."

"That's okay," I said. "I can't catch a fish, either."

I took the paddle and churned through the weeds to the inlet, where invisible currents opened a narrow channel through the blanket of vegetation. I pushed up into the brook. It meandered through a shadowed tunnel of overhanging maples, thickly walled with berry-bearing bushes. Little painted turtles plopped off logs ahead of us, and Sarah spied a big snapper lumbering along the shore. A black duck burst into flight ahead of the canoe. Warblers and catbirds flitted in the bushes. Here and there we saw the swirl of a feeding fish. The brook was too narrow and twisted for fly casting, but it was clear that the brook was alive.

As we turned a sharp elbow in the brook, I told Sarah, "This is the place where your brother caught his first trout." It had been ten years earlier. He had caught dozens of blue-gills and perch from the pond that day, too. The weeds had not been a problem.

We pushed farther and farther up into the brook, and it was still the way I remembered it. It flowed slowly but cold. The walls of brush and trees were entangled with grape vines and blooming wild roses. "It's so quiet," said Sarah. "It's like a jungle here. The Amazon or something."

After a mile or so a rocky riffle just inches deep forced us to turn around. As we returned to the spot where Michael had caught his trout, I saw a fish rise. It could be a trout, I thought. Probably not. I roll-cast toward it a few times. When I failed to entice a strike, I was tempted to believe that it had been, in fact, a trout. A bass or a bluegill would have taken a swipe at the fly.

Otherwise, we didn't bother trying to fish.

As we nosed the canoe onto the sand beach, a wagon was backing a trailered bass boat toward the water. Two young men got out, and one of them helped me hoist my canoe atop my car.

"Any luck?" he said, eyeing my fly rod.

I shook my head. "We were just out for a canoe ride."

"We never tried this place before," he said. "Guy told me there are bass in here."

I nodded. "Used to be, anyway."

"Big ones," he persisted, cocking an eye at me. "Like eight, ten pounds, huh?"

I shrugged. "I've heard that, yes."

They launched their boat, started up their trolling motor, and unlimbered their spinning rods.

Sarah and I waved to them. "Good luck," I called. And I meant it.

On the way home, Sarah said, "That was really fun. Can we do it again?"

"Sure," I said. "We'll try someplace else next time. Maybe we'll even catch a fish."

TWO

REAL
TROUT

REAL TROUT ARE BORN IN RIVERS. THEY HAVE SEX-
ually promiscuous parents who are also real trout. The odds
against a real trout attaining an inch in length are in the
neighborhood of one thousand to one.

Hatchery trout are not real trout.

There are some real trout in New England. I have encountered them in Vermont—a particularly large brown
that ate my Light Cahill on the Lamoille thirty years ago,
a pod of rainbows after dark on the Upper Connecticut,
flashes of quicksilver in Furnace Brook, a lone riser that I
cast to while Dad and Harold Blaisdell watched from the
highway bridge that spanned the White, peering straight
down at that trout and giving me a play-by-play.

I've found some real trout behind beaver dams in New
Hampshire, blood-spotted brookies, and in Maine lakes
and ponds where they're called squaretails.

When I was a kid I knew one brook in the common-
wealth of Massachusetts where I could find real trout. "Natives," we called them, and very few of them were six-inch
keepers. This brook now flows through suburban backyards
in a concrete trough of its very own.

Real trout should not be confused with carryover trout.
The latter are born in hatcheries, raised on pellets, and
dumped out of ten-gallon cans along with the prescribed
allotment of their kin into inhospitable water. Carryovers
somehow manage to avoid both eating scented marshmallows with hooks in them and dying from poisoned or over-
heated or oxygen-deficient or acidic or sterile water. Carryover trout, by definition, live through four seasons after
they are evicted from their nursery. They are freaks of the
hatchery genetic pool, where neither nature nor man dis-
criminates between the most and the least fit. All survive in

hatchery tanks. Carryovers survive in rivers. They are a little smarter or a little hardier or a little luckier than their brothers and sisters. Usually all three.

Carryover trout make worthy adversaries.

But they're not as worthy as real trout.

All real trout are smart and hardy and lucky. Otherwise they would not become the one in a thousand that survives to be an inch long.

Out West, most of the trout are real. And many of them grow to lengths of eighteen or twenty or more inches. By then you know they're *very* smart and *very* hardy (which are complementary qualities anyway), because luck alone wouldn't last that long.

I still don't know much about how to catch real trout. But I find that thinking about them occupies much of my consciousness, whether I'm in Massachusetts, where they're an abstraction and a memory, or Montana, where they're present in the rivers I'm wading and where other men obsess on them the same way I do.

4

Why the Big Ones Get Away

THE BIG RAINBOW WAS LYING EXACTLY WHERE HE should have been, in front of a Volkswagen-size boulder in the middle of the surging Box Canyon currents, and he crashed my marabou streamer just as it straightened on its down-and-across swing. This, I instantly realized, was not an average sixteen-to-eighteen-inch Box Canyon brute. This was one of the Box's fabled Big Ones, a rainbow shaped like an overinflated rugby ball, a six-, eight-, maybe a ten-pounder.

I wanted very badly to land him.

I lifted my fly rod high. My fish leaped once. Oh, my!

He lunged downstream. I held on. My reel screeched.

Then the line went slack.

I yelled an unprintable into the roar of the river's pounding currents and reeled in. Andy, fishing fifty yards upstream from me, called, "Big one?"

"Yeah," I answered. "He got away."

"Most of 'em do," he said.

It's a standing joke among us fishermen, of course, that the ones that get away are always big. But it's not funny when we consistently fail to land certified lunkers. And yet, as Andy pointed out, that's what usually happens.

It makes sense. Big fish are stronger, swifter, smarter. To fool them into eating our flies, we, ironically, typically need finer leader tippets and smaller flies. They test the extreme limits of both our skill and our equipment. They manage to find the weakest link, and they seem to know how to exploit it. We know we're lucky when we manage to defeat a Big One.

Truly big trout were an abstraction in my experience back East. A fourteen-inch hatchery stocker was, by eastern standards, big. I didn't know what big really meant until I began to travel in Montana and Idaho. I found myself abysmally unprepared for it.

I encountered my very first western Big One on the South Fork of the Snake River. He was a cutthroat of about twenty-two inches, and we spotted him cruising in the shadow of a sheer rock wall that had been painted white by generations of cliff swallows. Birdshit Pool, guide Doug Meyer called it. Doug showed me the fish, pointing out how he cruised in a circle on a radius of about fifteen feet, tipping up to eat every five or six feet. "Cast in his path," instructed Doug. "He'll eat it."

I did, and he did. I hauled back to set the hook. The line bow-and-arrowed back to me. The fly stayed in the fish's jaw.

Two days later I repeated my folly on a Hebgen Lake

gulper, a brown trout that Bob Lamm guessed would measure twenty-six inches.

Now, years later, I'm still doing it.

Big Ones, even in the West, are relatively scarce, and just getting one to strike is an achievement—usually, if we can admit it, a random blessing from the Red Gods. Playing trophy-size trout on a light fly rod requires special skills that most of us do not get to practice often enough to perfect.

And yet, if my experience is at all typical, we shouldn't blame ill fortune or even our own ineptitude for our failure to land those lunkers we are lucky enough to hook. Most of the Big Ones I've lost might have been landed had I simply adopted the right attitude.

I always go fishing *hoping* for a shot at a trophy. Yet rarely have I actually *believed* I'd hook into one.

The result is that I have been lazy and unprepared, and the Big Ones have unerringly found the weak link. Sometimes the soft place has been my inexperience in fighting monsters. Accustomed as I am to flabby eastern hatchery trout, I have failed to condition my reflexes to account for the strength, cunning, and speed of large native-born fish. When one of them takes my fly into his mouth, I tend to snub the line and yank back on the rod, a tactic that has worked fine on thousands of bluegills and ten-inch brookies. I know better. My heavy-handedness on those South Fork and Hebgen trout taught me that lesson. Its simple physics. Those two opposing forces—my hard strike in one direction, and a large trout swimming swiftly in the other direction—will snap a flimsy tippet every time. It would be depressing to know the number of Big Ones I've lost in our first instant of connection because, in my excitement and inexperience, I've set the hook too forcefully. I've learned (although I still fail to do it more often than not) that it takes only the gentlest tightening of the line to embed a small hook firmly into a trout's jaw. Even the surface tension of line bellied on the water will do it. You can hook a trout by lifting your rod and allowing the slack in your line hand to slide through the guides.

I know these things. Doing them, however, is another matter.

When a hooked Big One leaps free of the water, he will twist and jerk his head and try to fall onto the taut leader. Physics again. If you haul back on the rod when a Big One jumps, he will snap your tippet or tear the hook from his mouth. Give him slack line, however, and he loses his fulcrum. A leaping trout should be played just like a leaping tarpon: Bow to him.

And when he sets off on a long reel-screaming run, his power should be respected. Hold the rod high. Let him exhaust himself against the drag of the reel and the weight of the fly line. There's not much else you can do. Try to snub him down and he'll break you off.

I know all these things. I've lost plenty of Big Ones by failing to do them. I'd rather not keep blowing my opportunities, but I can still be philosophical about them. Some things can only be learned through repeated trials and errors. I figure I'll just have to keep practicing until I get it right. I can think of worse ways to spend my time.

So I can accept my inexperience and lack of skill. Most of my lost Big Ones, however, have resulted not from poor technique, but from equipment failure. And every one of those weak links in my gear was avoidable. I can't be so philosophical about the errors that common sense tells me I can prevent.

Fishermen, like baseball players, accept physical errors as part of the game. It's those mental errors, the errors of omission, that drive us crazy.

My vow this season is to think positively. I will assume the Big One will strike on every cast. I will Be Prepared.

During a lifetime of losing Big Ones, I have compiled a checklist of potential weak links. Each item on the list tells an agonizing tale of an escaped behemoth. Most of them are common sense. All of them, nevertheless, I have at one time or another ignored—to my chagrin.

DO NOT TRUST NEW HOOKS

The mouths of big fish of most species are constructed of bone, gristle, and tooth. It takes a sharp hook to penetrate beyond the barb and up to the bend. If the hook does not penetrate fully, it will pull out. You cannot assume that factory-new hooks, especially in the larger sizes, will come sharp enough. Some are duller than others. All should be honed before use, and periodically thereafter.

Test the temper of a new hook. If it's too brittle it can break in a fish's mouth. I busted off a large Bighorn River brown trout last summer—an event usually too common-place to report. But when I reeled in, I saw that the 5X tippet had held—it was the hook that broke at the bend!

If, on the other hand, the temper of the hook is too soft, it will bend open. That's what cost me that rugby-ball Box Canyon rainbow.

Check the eye of every new hook. Be sure it's completely

closed. Otherwise it can fray the leader or even allow the knot to slip loose.

If you tie your own flies, hone each hook before clamping it into your vise. And when the fly is completed, test its temper after removing it. A fly-tying vise can weaken or break hook points.

Do not hesitate to throw away imperfect hooks, before or after a fly is tied on it. It's cheaper than throwing away a Big One.

KEEP CHECKING YOUR HOOKS

If you nick a rock during a cast, check the hook immediately. I learned this the hard way one June afternoon while throwing streamers into the Winnipesaukee shoreline for smallmouths. One of my overenthusiastic casts bounced off a boulder and dropped into the water. A big bass grabbed it but came unhooked almost immediately. An hour and a dozen missed strikes later I stripped in to remove a string of weed from my fly. That's when I noticed that the point had broken off the hook.

Don't hesitate to change flies or lures, regardless of how hot that flawed one has been. A bent or broken point will not sink into the jaw of a Big One.

I've bent open the gap in hooks by snagging logs or by twisting the hook from a fish's mouth. This weakens it beyond repair. Bending it back into shape doesn't work. In the jaw of a Big One, it will spring open again.

Never tie on a fly when there is rust on the hook. A rusty hook is a weak hook. Moreover, a rusty eye will fray the leader tied to it, creating an instant weak link that your Big One will unerringly exploit.

KNOTS ARE THE WEAKEST LINKS

When you fail to land a Big One that you've hooked and played skillfully, you pray that you can lay it off to bad luck—a leader frayed by sharp teeth, a hook that simply pulls loose. When my first permit came off after a half-hour's struggle, that was my first thought. Please, Red Gods, don't show me a telltale little curl at the end of my empty leader.

But the Red Gods snorted mirthfully, and I had to confront the tragic reality that I had tied a bad knot, a knot that held for thirty minutes but refused to go another five. I've lost plenty of trout that way. But I may never come that close to a permit again.

I can't prove it, except from my own experience, but I would bet my Loomis 4-weight that more fish are lost because of bad knots than for any other reason. All knots are weaker than the line or leader they're tied with. There's no excuse for making them any weaker than they already are. Here are my three rules for strong knots:

1. Learn the best knots. You'll only need three: the improved clinch knot for tying leader to a straight-eye hook; the turle knot (be sure to tuck the tag end under the loop and to draw the loop around the shank of the hook behind the eye) for turned-up or turned-down eyes; and the double surgeon's knot for tying leader to leader (it's as strong as the blood knot, a lot easier to tie, and, unlike the blood knot, the surgeon's knot will join leader segments of significantly different diameters).

There are other useful knots worth learning—the Trilene knot (perhaps stronger than the improved clinch), the Duncan loop knot, the nail knot, and the surgeon's loop knot. For salt water you need an entirely different repertoire—the

Bimini twist, the Albright, the Homer Rhode loop. Accomplished fishermen know the best knot for every occasion, and they tie them with care.

2. Lubricate all your leader knots. After forming your knot, but before drawing it tight, dampen it in your mouth. Saliva is an excellent lubricant—just as good as the stuff you can buy for the purpose. Lubrication prevents the friction that weakens leaders, and also prevents slippage.

3. Test your knots. Tie them carefully, then pull on them firmly. It's irritating to have a knot come loose when you tug on it. But it's absolutely infuriating to discover that little curl at the end of your leader after a Big One has come loose.

4. Cheat. A drop of super glue on all but the knot that secures tippet to fly can neutralize a multitude of knot-tying sins.

THE CARE AND FEEDING OF LEADERS

I refuse to speculate on the number of large fish that have broken me off at wind knots. It's too embarrassing. Wind knots will happen, although most of the time it's the fly caster, not the wind, that causes them. A wind knot is a simple overhand knot cast into the leader. It creates an instant weak link. I can always tell when I have created a wind knot. This year I resolve to strip in, break off the wind knot, and retie my leader every time it happens. In past years I have been too lazy. In past years I have broken off too many large fish.

There are two other knots that can create break-offs: the knot that links your fly line to the leader, and the knot that connects the line to the backing. If these knots are bulky, or if they are not closely trimmed, they can snag in the guides long enough to pop the tippet. Tie them with the assumption that at some time you'll want them to slither slickly through the guides because a Big One insists on it. A well-tied nail knot or needle knot works best. Loop-to-loop connections are bulkier and have lost me a few Big Ones.

Whenever you have caught a fish, run the end of the leader through your fingertips, checking for nicks. Trout have teeth. Even toothless species such as bass have rough bony mouths that can fray a leader tippet. Follow the same precaution when your leader has rubbed against a rock or stump. Never hesitate to break off and retie frayed and weakened leaders.

Exposure to sunlight—or just plain old age—can weaken even unused tippet material. It took me three days of puzzling break-offs last summer during my Montana trout-bombing run to figure out that the spool of 6X I was using had a breaking strength of about six ounces. After I started using new tippets, I was forced to blame something else for the fish I lost.

REEL PROBLEMS

Bait casters and spin fishermen know the importance of their reels in playing fish. Fly fishermen, however, tend to regard the reel as simply a device for storing unused line—until they have to play a Big One.

Big fly-rod fish should be played off the reel. Don't skimp when you buy yourself a fly reel. Get one with a smooth, reliable drag. Fly fishermen should emulate their bait-casting and spinning cousins: Set the drag light enough to accommodate the tippet. It can always be cranked up a notch as the fish begins to tire.

Keep the gears lubricated. I was doing everything right when I hooked a trout named Mean Joe Green in the Frying Pan River. But as Mean Joe chugged across the pool with my shrimp fly hooked in the corner of his mouth, I noticed that the line was coming off my reel in erratic fits and starts. The reel sounded like a coffee grinder. The 5X tippet popped, of course, and Mean Joe finned back to his lair. That night I cleaned and oiled my reel, and the next day I landed Mean Joe's big brother.

Before each day's fishing, check all the screws in your reel. The time a loose screw will fall out and your reel will disintegrate is precisely when a Big One will be on the end of your line. And be sure the reel is seated firmly on the rod. I busted off one Belize bonefish in the middle of a screaming run when my reel fell off my rod, and another when the handle came unscrewed in my hand.

NET LOSSES

There are plenty of ways to land large fish without a net. I've had to try several of them because, in my eagerness to get fishing, I've forgotten my net or, hoping not to offend the Red Gods, I've purposely left it home.

Those other ways don't work as well as nets.

For smallish fish you don't necessarily need a net—and if you fail to land them, you don't feel too bad. To land a Big One, however, you're better off with a net—and one designed for the purpose. My beautiful antique teardrop-shaped net has scooped hundreds of little eastern brookies from New England streams, and even a few big (by eastern standards) browns. But when I took it out West, I quickly learned that a nine-by-fourteen inch net doesn't accommodate a twenty-two inch trout. One memorable Bow River Big One straddled the rim of my little net, refusing to sink into its bag. He flip-flopped, the fly snagged in the net's mesh, the leader popped, and I cursed. An insufficient net is no better than no net at all.

I've seen triumphant anglers scoop up Big Ones in their nets and then watch as the rotten mesh gave way, or a small hole ripped open and their trophy slid through, snapped the leader, and swam arrogantly away. Nets, like hooks, leaders, and reels, should be kept in tip-top repair if they're to do their jobs on lunker fish.

Attention to details such as these will not guarantee that you'll land every trophy you hook. You still need skill and luck. Awareness of all the things that can go wrong with hooks, knots, leaders, reels, and nets, however, is not a matter of skill or luck. It's just a matter of having the right attitude. Assume your next cast will draw a strike from your dream fish. Prepare for it. If you do end up losing him, you'll feel better knowing you did all you could.

But don't worry. You'll lose most of them anyway. There are lots of other things that can go wrong. Big Ones will always get away. Check with me next year. I guarantee that between us we'll come up with some new ways.

Stretching the Hatch

AROUND SIX IN THE EVENING LARGE TROUT BEGAN to bulge the placid surfaces of the Paradise Valley spring creek. I waited. Within a half-hour the first of the tiny yellow mayflies popped to the top of the water.

The spring-creek sulphur hatch had frustrated me in the past, but I was ready this time. I had tied half a dozen perfect imitations of the graceful duns—lemon body, sparse ginger hackle, perky grizzly-hackle-tip wings. I knotted a #20 onto my 7X tippet, fingered some Gink onto it, and floated it directly over the rainbow I had selected as my first victim. I could plainly observe him as he finned in the soft current, scrutinizing the flotsam that passed over him. Now he was feeding steadily.

My imitation appeared perfect to my eye. It was indistinguishable from the other duns that dotted the water's surface. It rode freely on the subtle currents at the end of the long fine leader. My chosen trout spied the elegant little fake, drifted under it, lifted casually to the surface—and ate something else less than six inches from my fly. I cast over him again. Again he selected something else to eat.

A dozen casts, the same result. I hunched over and cautiously waded closer, until I crouched not more than twenty feet from that trout. I had not spooked him. He continued to tilt his nose to the surface and suck in food. I could see the inside of his mouth wink white when he opened it to eat. I could distinguish every mark on him. I mentally measured him. Eighteen inches, minimum.

But I couldn't see what he was eating. I could only see that he was ignoring the little mayfly sailboats that dotted the water in favor of something else that remained, even from my close vantage point, invisible to me.

I shrugged, sighed, smiled. It had happened again. Another big trout too smart for me. I went looking for another.

In classic dry-fly fishing, the angler sits on the bank puffing his pipe, contemplatively awaiting the brief period in the life cycle of the mayfly when the nymphs have risen to the surface of the water and extricated themselves from their nymphal shucks. Then the angler springs into action. He attempts to "match the hatch" by tying on an imitation of the immature adult mayfly, the subimago. These duns, as fly fishermen call them, drift gracefully downstream and, according to the ancient ways, trout gluttonize on them and are suckers for anglers' well-cast imitations. The freshly hatched dun twists helplessly on the currents for a minute or two while its wings dry. Then, if a trout hasn't eaten it, it flies off the water to molt again. After an hour or so, all the duns have left the surface. The hatch is over. The dry-fly fisherman goes home.

It's great fun while it lasts. But it doesn't last long. And sometimes, as with my spring creek experience, the angler is skunked even while it's happening.

That was how I used to do it. Then I got a little smarter.

I tried to arrive before the hatch. I bumped weighted nymphs along the bottom while I waited for it. When the little sailboats began bobbing down the stream, I tied on the closest imitation I had and gave it my best shot. And after the last dun fluttered off the water, I tied on a nymph again.

I began to catch more fish.

It took me a long time to realize that I was still missing my best bets.

There are three distinct phases of the mayfly's life, plus a transitional time. Trout feed on them during all stages. The dun phase is the briefest, and it's the time when the mayfly, because at any moment it may fly away (I wonder if that's where the mayfly got its name?), is least vulnerable to feeding trout. It's ironic that this is traditionally the target time for the dry-fly fisherman.

Trout eat avidly on the surface during two other stages in the mayfly's life—the emergence, that transition period when the nymphs float or swim to the surface and molt into duns, and the spinner fall, the time after the adult imagoes have fallen spent from their mating exertions to the water's surface, ultimately to die.

As a hardheaded Yankee doubter, I assumed for a long time that effete anglers created a mythological bug they called the "emerger" either to dupe unwary browsers in fly shops or to rationalize their failures to catch rising trout. "They won't eat my dun," they would say. "Must be keying on emergers."

I always figured the fish wouldn't eat *my* dun because it was the wrong size or color, or, as hard as it was for me to conceive of it, because I wasn't fishing it with the necessary subtlety.

My hardheadedness gave me several seasons of frustration. But I have learned that if you fish long enough, eventually you'll do something wrong that produces a revelation.

One July evening several summers ago, Andy and I waded into a pale morning dun hatch on the Missouri River downriver from my favorite Montana town, Wolf Creek (pronounced "crick"). Pretty little orange-bodied duns were popping to the surface and trout were slurping. It looked like easy pickin's.

It wasn't, of course. I kept changing flies. They all looked pretty good to my eye, but the fish didn't agree. I got a few halfhearted refusals.

I changed flies for the fourth or fifth time, Ginked it up, and cast it over a steady riser. The fly did not ride perky on its hackle tips. It just sogged there in the surface film. I realized what had happened. Back in January when I was tying my season's PMD collection, some heavy-wire nymph hooks had gotten mixed in with my dry-fly batch.

But before I could strip it in and change flies, a trout ate it. With my rod pleasantly bowed, I called over to Andy, "Dumb fish took it wet."

"Aha!" he said instantly. "They're on emergers." Andy, I am frequently forced to admit, is smarter than I.

I caught half a dozen trout on that ill-conceived dry fly. I discovered that giving it a little twitch as it approached a feeding trout increased the chances of its being eaten. The soggier and more bedraggled it became, the better the fish liked it.

I began that day with a mistake. I ended it with an insight.

I remembered that Paradise Valley spring creek rainbow—and dozens just like him—that had ignored not only my best dun imitation, but real duns as well. He was feeding selectively, I retrospectively decided, on either floating nymphs or half-emerged duns. Had I greased my leader and dipped a nymph of the appropriate size into dry-fly floatant, I might have caught that trout.

In fact, I have done just that many times since. I am now a devoted emerger fisherman.

Before mayfly duns actually appear on the water, trout will begin to "rise," an indication that the hatch has begun. Fly fishermen mistake their bulges and swirls for surface feeding. In fact, these rising trout are eating nymphs and emergers in or just beneath the surface film. They will ignore traditional dun patterns, but an old-fashioned wet fly (or a sunken dry fly) twitched just under the surface is a workable imitation of the emerging mayfly as it struggles toward the surface. Even after the duns begin to pop onto the top of the water, trout will often ignore them in favor of the more vulnerable emerging subimagoes. Floating nymphs do the trick in the early stages of the emergence, while imitations of incompletely hatched duns will fool even the wariest trout as the emergence proceeds and duns begin to appear on the water.

Westerners will argue that the pickiest trout in the world

inhabit their hard-fished spring creeks. We easterners will gladly match the IQs of the trout that live in some of our urban streams—the Farmington River, outside Hartford, Connecticut, for example, or the Swift, in central Massachusetts, two of my favorites—against any trout in Montana or Idaho. I've fished them all and been frustrated on all of them. But by focusing on floating nymph and emerger patterns before and during mayfly hatches, I've managed to catch my share of trout—and it all happens on the surface where I like it best.

Any unweighted nymph can be made to float by treating it with dry-fly floatant. Even better are floating nymphs designed especially for the early stages of mayfly emergences. I make mine by tying standard nymph patterns on dry-fly hooks and adding a couple of turns of hackle over the thorax, which I clip flush with the bottom. By cutting all the wing and hackle material off a standard dun pattern, I have created passable floating nymphs in emergencies.

Poorly tied dry flies, like the one I used on the Missouri, will catch trout keyed on emergers when well-tied ones won't. Emerger imitations work even better. The key, I believe, is to drift it in—not on—the surface film.

The emerger patterns I've found most deceptive are part nymph and part dun, representing the incompletely molted subimago. A short bunch of brown or olive yarn or marabou, half the body length, at the tail suggests the trailing nymphal shuck. The body color matches that of the dun. I use just a wisp of hackle, either tied parachute-style or trimmed flush with the bottom so that the fly floats in, not atop, the surface film. A little stub of poly yarn or wood duck breast feather to represent the wing case completes the fly. I have been surprised how often the trout that steadfastly refuse to take my standard dun patterns will readily eat emerger imitations during all stages of the hatch. Perhaps they know that duns might fly away at any moment but emergers are helpless. Trout seem to prefer them.

Sometimes I find myself without the right emerger pattern in my box. Then I simply hack the bottom hackles off the standard dun pattern and clip the wings to a short nub. If I can get it to float low, or drift just beneath the surface, this makeshift emerger usually fools trout.

Before the hatch brings trout to the surface, I fish either the nymph or the emerger like a wet fly, casting across and downstream and twitching it back. Once the duns begin to pop onto the surface, I drift the nymph, then the emerger, dry and drag-free over bulging or sipping trout. Sometimes I will continue this way throughout the hatch. At other times, I'll gladly switch to a standard dun pattern. The trout tell me what to do.

After the last dun has either been eaten or has lifted off the water to molt for its final time, the "hatch" is over. But for the trout, one of their favorite mealtimes has yet to arrive. Next on their menu are the spinners.

The life of an imago—a sexually mature adult mayfly, whose characteristic airborn mating dance gives it the name "spinner"—varies by species. Rarely is it more than twenty-four hours. The spinner fall is usually triggered by cool temperatures—late afternoon in the early season, and nighttime later in the year, although stormy weather will delay the mating and hence the time when the spinners return to the water to die. Typically, the spinners of a morning hatch fall at dusk, while those of an afternoon hatch will fall to the water early the following morning.

Often the hatches come irregularly throughout the day, so that spinners and emerging duns litter the water at the same time, in which case the angler must closely observe the feeding trout to determine what they have selected to eat. More often than not it will be the easy-to-catch spinners. When feeding on duns, trout tend to boil and slash at the living insects, sensing, perhaps, that they might fly away at any moment. They usually sip the dead or dying spinners casually, barely lifting their noses above the water and sucking them in, as if they know that their prey cannot escape. Just to confuse us, trout suck emergers off the surface with identical riseforms. Experimentation and careful observation will enable the angler to solve this problem.

A spinner fall will often last significantly longer than the hatch that precedes it, as fallen imagoes from all points upstream pass over a given trout's lair. On the Missouri River in the summer, Trico spinners reliably blanket the water early every morning. Trout eat them well into the afternoon. I've fished Blue-Winged Olive spinners virtually the entire day on the Bighorn. On my eastern streams in the springtime, the Hendrickson spinners begin to fall in late afternoon. Good fishing to them continues as far into dark as the angler is willing to stay.

Once it has fallen onto the water, the spinner looks like a tiny airplane. It's characterized by its translucent wings that typically rest on the surface in a spent position. Its tail is longer than that of its dun counterpart, and in many species its body color changes from its dun shade into a brown or rusty hue. Most experts believe that trout key on the way light filters through the spinner's wings. Sparse white or gray hackle, wound on as for a conventional dry fly and then clipped top and bottom, works well for wings, as do hen-hackle tips and poly yarn. In any case, the spinner is inert. Its body lies flush on the water, not upright and perky like the dun.

An emergency spinner imitation can be fashioned streamside from a standard dun pattern simply by clipping a V of hackle and the wings out of the top of the fly and trimming off the bottom hackle. If the body color and size are close, and if it floats low on the water, it will take trout.

By fishing the earliest moments of the hatch—the period when mayfly duns are beginning to emerge—through the traditional dun stage and into the spinner fall, the end of the insect's life cycle, I've had days of almost continuous surface activity. Stretching the hatch certainly beats sitting on the bank puffing a pipe and waiting for capricious trout to decide if they're going to eat duns.

6

Bank Shots

"LOOK AT THOSE GUYS!" MUTTERED DAVE. "WADING right through the fish. Unbelievable!"

Andy and I were sitting on the banks of the Bighorn with guides Dave Schuller and Bill Rohrbacher, trying to catch a little relief from the blazing Montana midday sun in the shade of a scraggly cottonwood. The soft beginnings of the afternoon blow dried the sweat as it formed on our foreheads.

The guides had selected the site for the view, and we had been gazing upstream watching a lineup of rising trout. They were rhythmically poking their noses out of the slick band of shallow water against the bank. There must have been a hundred of them. Once in a while Dave would point at a particularly big nose and mumble around a mouthful of lunch, "That one. A real toad." It was an awesome sight. Black trout heads everywhere. In the Montana quiet we could hear them slobber and slurp.

So we sat and watched and anticipated. We munched Dave's thick antelope-salami sandwiches and sipped lemonade. We were in no particular hurry. We knew the trout would be feeding there all afternoon.

Our two driftboats were tucked against the bank downstream from where we sat. We were inconspicuous in the high grass under the cottonwood. So when the new boat veered shoreward and was beached fifty yards upriver from us, we couldn't accuse its occupants of poaching on our place. And it wasn't that all of those rising trout in the shallow flatwater stopped feeding the instant the new boat arrived that irritated Dave. We could always find more fish.

"Sheer, utter ignorance," he observed sadly.

Bill mumbled something less printable.

The three men stepped out of their boat, fly rods in hand. They sloshed through the calf-deep water where our trout had been feasting and waded out to their waists in the heavy main currents of the Bighorn. Bracing themselves against the powerful flow, they began to cast. They were skilled. They achieved admirable distance. They double-hauled expertly.

"It's really strange," said Dave. "Guys fishing from boats, they cast as close into shore as they can. But when they get out of their boat and start wading, they go up to their armpits and heave it out toward the middle." He shrugged. "Who can account for human nature?"

Bill offered a few suggestions.

We watched the three fly casters. They stuck it out for about twenty minutes. None of them had a strike. Then they splashed back through the shallow water, climbed into their driftboat, and floated past us.

Fifteen minutes later, black noses began to reappear in the bankside flatwater.

The four of us spent most of the afternoon with those trout. We worked our slow way upstream through the lineup, taking turns. We waded side by side on our knees in the foot-deep water, keeping our profiles low. We used 6X tippets and the guides' version of the Blue-Winged Olive spinner, which they call the Green Meanie. We made short casts, twenty or thirty feet, no more. Perfect casts—three feet upstream and directly over a trout's nose—usually induced a strike.

Imperfect casts—just a couple inches off to one side or the other, or too far upstream, or not far enough—invariably produced nothing.

A sloppy cast put down the fish.

They were all brown trout in that lineup. Big ones, even by Bighorn standards. Nineteen and twenty inches. We busted off a couple even bigger ones, trout with noses the size of garden toads.

Dave and Bill were still grumbling when we finally waded back to our boat. "They do it all the time," Dave said. "People who don't understand trout, can't read a river. Hard to believe. Can't they *see* all those snouts poking up? I guess it's because they're not looking, not expecting it. They think big trout want the big water, and they think big trout make big splashes when they rise. So that's where they look. And they miss the best of it. I see it all the time here. All the boats, they go cruising right past the choicest parts of the river."

"Not to complain," grinned Bill through his beard. "More for us. But damn!—" he waved his hand at the ten-foot-wide band of flatwater against the bank inside the swifter current.—"*This* is what trout like. They can lie here in comfort, not fighting the river, their bellies on the bottom, and they just tilt up at their ease to sip whatever comes their way on the surface."

"Like you said," observed Andy. "All the better for us."

There are times on big rivers, both East and West, when weighted nymphs drifted through riffles and along the edges of deep swift currents produce large fish for me. And sometimes I like to wade deep and throw streamers as far as my crude double haul will permit. But when its dry-fly action I want—which is most of the time—I apply the lesson Dave Schuller and Bill Rohrbacher taught me on the Bighorn. I go bank shooting.

Focusing on the narrow bands of soft water near the banks has saved me from being overwhelmed by the size and complexity of big water, from New England's Deerfield and Connecticut and Housatonic to the Missouri and Yellowstone and Snake out West. Now I can step confidently into new rivers for the first time and find feeding fish. I simply ignore the bigness of strange water and concentrate on those rivers-within-rivers that flow slowly against the banks.

Small trout waters are just like big ones, except, if you'll excuse me, for their size. They contain the same complexity of currents, the same combinations of holding water and barren water, as do their outsized counterparts. On western spring creeks and eastern freestone streams alike, I have learned to study the cushions of water against the banks. On small rivers, those cushions may only be a foot wide, trout like to lie with their sides almost brushing the bank and sip only inches from it. Spring-creek bank-sippers, for example, tend to lie smack against logjams or in the shadow of an overhanging tuft of grass in water barely deep enough to cover their backs. Their delicate riseforms are easy to miss. They resemble the disturbance you'd make by dropping a BB onto the water. Don't be fooled. These are often large fish.

In my opinion, bank shooting is the most challenging— and rewarding—of all forms of dry-fly fishing. The challenge is more to the angler's streamcraft, stealth, patience, and attention to detail than to his technical skills. Anybody with modest fishing ability can learn to take bank-feeding trout. But you've got to be a good hunter.

Bank-sippers tend, for some reason, to be larger trout. These fish don't grow big by ignoring hints of danger. They know about herons, ospreys, mink—and fishermen. In slow-moving skinny water it doesn't take much to spook a feeding trout. They know they're exposed, so they remain correspondingly more alert. The flash of a fly line in the sun, the spatter of water from a false cast, the shadow of a passing sparrow, the wave put up by a stumbling fisherman—all send trout scurrying to midriver sanctuary. Delicate casting and stealth are keys to stalking bank-feeders successfully.

Nor, in the smooth slow water next to the banks, are feeding trout heedless about what they eat. Foodstuffs drift toward them slowly and in great abundance. Anything tied to a leader tippet must look edible. It cannot drag, however slightly, and it must pass directly through their feeding lanes or they will not eat it. No matter how many trout are feeding and how closely packed they seem to be, the trick is to pick a single fish and cast specifically to him. Flockshooting is useless. Long fine tippets and absolutely pin-point casting are mandatory.

So here's the picture: You've found a dense pod of trout noses poking rhythmically out of the water within a yard of the bank in water barely calf-deep. You wade hunched over, or preferably on your knees. You pick out a single feeding trout and ignore all the others. You make sure that your leader's long, fine, and well balanced. You false-cast to the side to keep the shadow and spatter off your chosen fish. You gauge the feeding rhythm of your trout, timing your cast so that your fly will reach him when he's ready to lift his nose to eat. You aim a yard directly upstream of him. Your fly may be too small to distinguish among the dozens of naturals around it. But if you've cast well, whether you can see your fly on the water or not, you'll set the hook when your trout rises. Sometimes—often—you'll find yourself tied to a very large fish.

On smaller streams the game is slightly different. Bank-sippers there tend to be loners, and the preferred approach is usually from midstream, casting across and down. Long drag-free floats are difficult this way, since you must lay your line across several different currents. Stealthy approaches, long fine leaders, and short casts minimize this problem.

Sounds too hard, you say? Sounds too highly refined? Better stick to the easier fish in the swifter currents until you get better with the fly rod, eh?

Wait. Without minimizing the challenges of bank shoot-ing—and what fun would fishing be anyway if it weren't challenging?—I believe that anybody with average fly-fishing skills can take more and bigger dry-fly trout this way than by tackling the heavy currents. If you can make

short, accurate casts—and anybody can, with practice—
you can bank on consistently good dry-fly fishing.

I'm average, at best. I can do it.

Anybody can learn stealth. Go slow, stay low, study the
water. Learn to spot those inconspicuous little dimpling
rises. Ease into position. Make your first cast count.

And anybody can equip himself properly. Well-balanced
outfits that will cast a short, straight, accurate line aren't
necessarily the most expensive. Don't be intimidated by
slender tippets. The 6X they make nowadays is amazingly
strong. Go long and fine and use a rod that will put the fly
where you aim it.

You'll find bank-feeders eating off the surface when it
seems that all the other trout in the river are sulking near
bottom. I have consistently enjoyed excellent dry-fly fishing
at midday while most of the other anglers on the river were
sitting on the banks waiting for the next hatch. Bank-
sippers, I have found, tend to be opportunistic feeders. In
the absence of an established hatch, they eat whatever bugs
come their way. I've had particularly good luck with terrestrials—beetles and ants—but I've done about as well with
an assortment of small mayfly imitations regardless of prevailing insect activity. A #18 or #20 Royal Wulff or Adams
works fine if it can be drifted naturally over a bank-sipper.
Rarely is fly pattern the important variable in catching
bank-feeding trout. It's all in the approach and the presentation.

All trout, whether they're feeding in midriver currents or
in skinny water near the bank, tend to set up stations. They
rise in one place and don't like to move very far for their
food. Locating their stations precisely is necessary. In the
choppy surfaces of undifferentiated big water, pinpointing

the location of a feeding trout is difficult. With bank-feeders, however, it's easy, because you have several points of reference—eight inches out and a foot down from a trailing branch, for example, or just inside the tiny lick of current flowing around a boulder. Additionally, in shallow water you can often see the shape of your target ghosting just under the surface. Cast your fly a yard above him. Watch him as he spots it, flicks his tail, drifts under it, lifts his snout open-mouthed to suck it in. Resist the impulse to strike too early, if you can.

Hatch or not, I can usually count on finding a few bank-sippers to work on. Many of my angling days in eastern and western rivers of all sizes have been salvaged by a half-dozen memorable stalks of quiet-water trout during times when the other fishermen were proclaiming the river dead.

Bank shooting combines the best parts of hunting as well as fishing, which is probably why it's the kind of fishing I like the most. Each fish is a challenge. It's head-to-head, just that single fish and me alone on the river, and I don't mind spending an hour or more trying to cåtch him. And no matter which of us wins, the hunt provides me with another memory. As Dave Schuller says, it's money in the bank.

THREE

THE END OF
THE LINE

WHEN I RHAPSODIZE ABOUT FISHING (AS I USUALLY do, since there isn't much else in the world I can honestly rhapsodize about) to people who don't do it, they usually observe, "Well, I used to fish a little when I was a kid, but I guess I just don't have the patience for it anymore."

Actually, I don't either, at least not for their concept of it. Fishing, in fact, is pretty maniacal the way Andy and I usually do it, and we have agreed that patience is more of a vice than a virtue in fly fishing for trout.

Still, once in a while I like to harken to my roots and tap into my dwindling reservoir of patience.

A warm April afternoon still lures me to a spot on the sunny side of Walden or White Pond. I roll-cast a worm into the water, strip a few feet of line from my reel, and prop my fly rod on a forked stick driven into the ground. I lean my back against a tree trunk. The spring sun bathes my face and tempts me to close my eyes. I'd do it, except I don't want to miss the sudden quiver of life out there where my line enters the water, the quick twitch-pause-twitch, then the slither of the line through the guides.

It's lazy fishing, old-fashioned boy-with-a-pole fishing. It requires patience, and a capacity for daydreaming, and it tugs my mind back to a day when time was my most expendable resource and I expended it extravagantly on the banks of watery places. It's good to be reminded of such days.

I still like to drift a worm against the undercut banks of Beaver Brook in New Hampshire where little native brookies live, too. Once or twice a summer I'll take off my shoes, roll up my pant legs, and hand-capture a dozen crawfish. Then a willing child and I will paddle out to a dropoff, and we'll lower our bait down to where the smallmouths are lurking. I still get a kick out of seeing a bobber dance on a bluegill pond, and casting Jitterbugs on a July evening against the lily pads on Bare Hill Pond, and heaving Rapalas into the moonlit surf on Cisco Beach.

As the years have passed, these have become important ceremonial activities for me. I want to keep in touch with my memories. I need periodic reminders.

Increasingly, though, I find that all I want is a fly rod in my hand.

I want to wade on my knees in foot-deep water until I can drop a Crazy Charlie near a school of tailing bonefish. I want to float a sulphur emerger I invented myself over a humping spring creek brown trout. I want to bounce a deer-hair bug into a dark place under the shoreline bushes where a four-pound largemouth lives. I want to double-haul a Deceiver into the middle of a school of slashing blues in the mouth of the Merrimack. I want to twitch a black rubberlegs for bluegills, strip a chartreuse Woolly Worm for crappies, drift a caddis pupa for a river land-locked salmon, slam a big yellow bucktail up into the weeds where a pike might lurk.

Patience has no relevance for these pursuits.

There are other ways to catch fish. Sometimes a fly is the only thing a fish will eat—try persuading a midging rainbow to hit a Mepps spinner or a salmon egg. Sometimes a fly rodder is downright handicapped. Usually, in my experience, a competent fly fisherman can hold his own with spin casters or bait fishermen.

It doesn't really matter. I prefer the fly rod neither for the extra challenge nor for its special effectiveness. It doesn't have anything whatsoever to do with catching fish.

I like fly casting. I like the sense of control, the absence of mechanics intervening between me and the fly. I like the delicate precision, the poetic rhythm, the beautiful unfolding of the loop over the water. Fly casting is quiet and intimate. No clicks, clanks, whirrs, or splashes are heard—just the sibilant swish of line moving through air.

I love the fish that eat flies. Especially trout. I love their colors and their shapes. I love the way their mouths wink white when they eat a nymph and the way their noses lift to sip an emerger from the surface film. And I love the places where they live—a Paradise Valley spring creek, a Pennsylvania limestoner, a Cape Cod kettle pond, a western freestoner such as the Madison, a tailwater like the Bighorn or the Green. I see beauty in the things trout eat—is there anything in nature more perfect than a natural pale morning dun drifting on tippy-toes along a current seam toward a waiting brown trout?

Put a fly rod into my hand and something I have created myself on the end of my line. I'm a happy man.

7

Gulpers in the Smoke

EVERY NIGHT THE EASTERN SKYLINE GLOWED orange. Sometimes from the streets of West Yellowstone we could see flames licking at the sullen, starless, sooty sky over the Park.

New platoons of firefighters arrived every day, combat-toughened troops from the Pacific Northwest, Indians from Arizona and New Mexico, college-age kids from all over the country. They got an even more hospitable reception than usual from the local shopkeepers and innkeepers and restaurateurs.

They had come to save the town.

Those burdened with such decisions kept closing, then reopening, the roads through the Park. On some days you could drive to Old Faithful and Buffalo Ford. On other days giant fingers of flame poked across the roads and leaped from treetop to treetop ahead of the prevailing wind, and tourists and fishermen were barred. Herds of elk, driven from the mountains, grazed on the well-manicured lawns in Canyon Village and Mammoth. Buffalo bedded in the dusty roads.

The last rainfall had come on Mother's Day. Now it was late August. The forests were tinder-dry. The lodgepole pines, the predominant trees, were old and diseased, and they flamed up like paper.

The fires—for there were many of them, and the larger ones were given names like battlefields—flared up in unpredictable spots. Many different areas burned at the same time, some of them containing several square miles. Flames and embers leaped into the sky, flew on the ever-present winds, and landed to ignite another section. From the air, Yellowstone Park was an erratic quilt of black patches edged with orange and surrounded by green, all overlaid with thick gray smoke.

In the Totem Cafe, where Andy and I hung out after each day's fishing, debates over the let-burn policy of the park administration were decidedly one-sided. Discussions narrowed to fireighting tactics and weaponry—bulldozers versus explosives versus backfires versus water and foam. Nobody wanted the Park to burn. Nobody wanted West Yellowstone to go up in flames.

It seemed as if it might. There was talk of evacuation.

Each day the weather forecast was the same. Cloudless skies. Temperatures in the nineties. Gusty Montana winds, as always. Chance of precipitation: Zero.

In New England, the weatherman *never* dares predict a zero chance of precipitation.

Andy and I fished by day. We did not venture into the Park. We stalked trout heads on the Railroad Ranch, stripped leech imitations over the weed beds on Henry's

Lake, floated the Box, waded the Madison near the Grizzly Bar and behind the Slide Inn. By day we caught trout, and in the high white August sun we saw no flames. The smell of smoke was so pervasive that our senses soon dulled and stopped registering it.

We fished hard every day and didn't think about the fires.

But after dark, every night, the reality of the fires returned to us. The smoke hung heavier over the West Yellowstone streets than over the waters we fished. We could even smell it in the fly shops and restaurants. And we could see the orange skyline, and sometimes the licking flames.

The Totem bartender and waitresses served us nightly updates with our gin and tonics and ribeye steaks. Four miles west of town. Now three miles. One day the wind shifted and seemed to be pushing the flames away. Then it shifted again and they closed the west entrance to the Park. Another two hundred fighters were flown in from Oklahoma. The upper meadow at Slough Creek was scorched. Bureaucrats continued to debate policy abstractions two thousand miles away, back in D.C. Some folks on the edge of town were piling their belongings into pickup trucks and fleeing. Zero chance of rain in the long-range forecast.

We had hoped to cast to gulpers on Hebgen Lake. In August the Trico spinners fall onto the water at dawn, and soon after sunrise the *Callibaetis* come off, and until the wind comes up, big browns and rainbows cruise the surface and can be taken on dry flies.

It was difficult and unpredictable, high-risk high-reward dry-fly fishing, and Andy and I hated the thought of missing it.

Usually the wind over the plains lies down until around

noontime. But in that summer of 1988 the wind seemed to blow all day and all night. In the Park it fueled the existing fires and blew flaming embers to new fire sites. On Hebgen Lake it blew the bait off the water. There is no gulper fishing in the wind.

Finally, with only three days left in our West Yellowstone fishing sojourn, Andy and I agreed. We'd get to Hebgen at dawn the next morning and try it. If we got blown off the lake, we'd have lost only a few hours of sleep.

We got up at five and smelled the smoke, thicker and more acrid than ever. Outside, the darkness was absolute. And when we finned away from shore in our tubes an hour later it was still dark, and the smoke burned our eyes.

The surface of the water was black and fuzzy and still as we paddled backward across the narrow arm of the lake toward the cliffs where the rainbows come out to eat. Andy and I moved along side by side, within an easy cast of each other. I could barely make out his silhouette in the thick smoky darkness.

We didn't talk, respecting, I suppose, the eerie shrouded stillness of the lake. Then Andy whispered, "There's one!" And a moment later, louder this time, he said, "Another. They're gulping!"

I squinted into the murk and I began to see them. Trout were feeding all around me. Gulpers don't lift to the surface, eat once, then sink back. Instead they remain up and feed several times in succession. Usually you see the rise, then another close by, then another, and you judge the trout's path and cast your fly to the spot where you estimate he will feed next. Sometimes the trout actually move across the surface of the water with the tops of their heads breaking the skin of the lake and their mouths chomping, and they look like incompletely submerged submarines.

Some of those trout in Hebgen look as big as submarines, too. They run, typically, eighteen to twenty inches long. I have busted off gulpers several inches longer than that.

The first time Bob Lamm took Andy and me gulpering, I started by dropping my fly directly into the bull's-eye of the rise. Bob quickly corrected me. "That's the worst place to cast," he said. "Think about it. It's a river through the looking glass. This is still water. It doesn't carry food to the fish. The bugs are just sitting there. It's the fish that are flowing, not the water. A stationary trout is a starving trout. They've got to move to eat. So what's the one place where a fish won't be?"

I nodded. "Sure. The place where he just was."

So the trick was to judge by one or two successive rises where the trout would decide to eat next. Bob needed to see only a single rise to tell. He paddled in his tube beside me, and when a fish gulped within casting range he'd say, "To the right," or, "Coming this way, seven o'clock."

I didn't do very well following his instructions, but after watching large fish gulping all around me for a while I began to see what he was seeing. I could distinguish the trout's head from his tail, and I learned to predict his path from the way he swirled after eating, and I began to get my fly into his sight.

When casting to stationary trout in moving water, the trick is to land the fly upstream of the fish on the particular current that will float it down to him. You *know* an accurate cast will bring your fly to the fish. Casting to moving trout in still water is river fishing in reverse, with the additional uncertainty created by the trout's free will. He doesn't necessarily cruise in a straight line and eat every seven feet. He may come to the top, gulp along for ten or fifteen feet, then sink back under the surface to chew his food and ponder his fate. He may decide to take a left turn, or to move in erratic zigzags, or to reverse his direction.

So you make your best guess. You try to lead your target trout by ten or fifteen feet so he'll have a chance to see your fly and decide it's good to eat. And then you watch your fly with one eye and the trout with the other, and you wait. If you've guessed well, you can see the distance between fish and fly close down. You triangulate, and you anticipate the intersection.

Gulper fishing is nerve-wracking.

On a good morning of gulper fishing Andy and I have landed and released half a dozen big trout apiece.

The standard Adams in #16 imitates the *Callibaetis* that we usually find on Hebgen in the morning. We use 5X tippets. Gulpers are not particularly selective or leader-shy. They will eat if they find your fly at the place where they intend to pause for a bite.

I have occasionally found trout gulping midges on Cape Cod trout ponds in April. I make the two-hour drive when I awaken to a soft, misty, absolutely still day. Then I like to twitch midge pupa imitations just under the surface across the bow of my chosen fish. I have even caught a few on midge drys, Hebgen-style.

I have seen trout cruising the weedy shallows in lakes eating damselflies or scuds or mayfly nymphs. They are not gulping, but you can see them move and the principle is similar: Guess their route, cast quickly and accurately, and anticipate the intersection of fish and fly.

Gulping behavior is not unique to the trout of Hebgen. Wherever stillwater trout key on aquatic insects, a big hatch and the right conditions will often—but not always—bring them to the surface. In lakes and ponds where the fish feed primarily on leeches or baitfish, however, I have never found them gulping.

Hebgen Lake is one place where you can absolutely count on finding gulpers on an August morning—if there's no wind.

On that particular August morning in 1988 there was no wind on Hebgen. Nor did we see the sun rise that day. Andy and I fished together. We talked conversationally, exchanging running commentary. Sometimes we quietly cursed the whimsical unpredictability of the fish. We repeatedly marveled at the odd sense of disorientation and isolation we felt out there on the lake, suspended on the membrane of the water, our bottom halves immersed in the water and our top halves encased in that inversion of thick, still smoke.

"Dante's fifth circle," Andy muttered once.

"Hellish," I agreed. "Except for all the fish."

Our voices seemed to carry louder through the smoky medium, and we didn't have to speak loudly to be heard. I could hear Andy as if he were at my elbow. Yet I could barely see him. He was a shadow, a blurry shape in the thick smoke that hung over Hebgen that morning.

The fearsome Yellowstone fires had, ironically, blessed us. They gave us the perfect conditions for gulper fishing: Heavy overcast and absolutely still air. The bugs and the trout didn't know the difference between clouds and smoke.

At midday the sun was a blurred copper penny above us. It cast no shadow, nor did it burn away the smoke.

The wind lay abed all day. The *Callibaetis* hatched all day. The gulpers gulped all day. Andy and I caught trout all day. We quit around five, only because we hadn't eaten for twelve hours and because we had caught two days' worth of trout. Twelve or fifteen apiece, we figured, though neither of us had counted. We'd busted off about as many as we'd landed, and we'd raised and failed to hook that many, too.

It was a singular, unforgettable day of fishing. And when we relived it that night over prime rib at the Totem, we agreed that if it took the burning of Yellowstone Park to give us our best day of gulpering, we'd have been happy to settle for an average morning of fishing.

A thunderstorm blew through that night. The great cracks and booms awakened us, and through the window we watched the lightning inscribe brilliant zigzags across the big sky and light up the plains. Hailstones the size of Globugs clattered on the roof.

The next morning the sky was again cloudless and clear and the wind was blowing. The fires were still devouring the Park, undaunted by the night's quick, futile downpour.

We fished the Henry's Fork for our last two days in Montana.

A few weeks after we returned to Massachusetts I read that a September snowstorm had finally accomplished what hundreds of firefighters and millions of heated words had failed to do. Mother Nature, once again, had the final say.

When we drove through Yellowstone Park the following summer, we found emerald western grasses blanketing the hills and vast beds of pastel and neon wildflowers rioting on the sun-soaked meadows and among the angular shadows cast by stands of blackened trees. Tourists and trout fishermen had invaded West Yellowstone in their usual numbers.

There was a sense that the tourists had come to view a corpse, but the fishermen were there just to cast flies to trout.

And in the Totem Cafe, the bartender talked of caddis and sulphur hatches and how well the fish were taking nymphs on the Madison. Yes, the gulpers were eating *Callibaetis* on Hebgen, he said. Andy and I tried it one morning. We got there at sunrise and caught three or four apiece before the wind came up. It was exactly what we had hoped for.

8

Fly-Tying Season

THE SMELLS—BUCKTAILS AND HACKLE NECKS AND mothballs and head cement—are still evocative for me today. The materials had poetic names—tinsel and floss and chenille, jungle cock and peacock and golden pheasant, teal and mallard and wood duck, blue dun and ginger and grizzly.

Dad ceremonially set up his fly-tying table in the living room on New Year's Day, and he plied his art just about every winter evening thereafter. I'd pull up a chair by his elbow to watch him tie while the "I Love Lucy Show" laugh track played in another corner of the room.

After dinner he laid out the materials for the evening, and I learned that the brown bucktail and the skein of yellow chenille signified an evening of Dark Tigers, whereas the grizzly and ginger necks and the wood-duck breast feathers meant that a dozen or two identically perfect Near-enufs would magically emerge from Dad's vise. When he took out the big hooks and the deer-hair skins, I knew it would be an evening of what he called "hedge-clipping"— spinning hair and shaping bass bugs.

Dad supplied all of his friends with flies, and since he had many friends, he had to tie hundreds of flies, and flies for every season. He approached fly tying as a manufacturing process, and he called it a craft. But to me, what he did was an art, and the pieces he created were beautiful—perfectly symmetrical and proportioned, sweetly tapered, subtly colored.

As the winter nights passed, his boxes filled with flies. There were few evenings when Dad didn't put in a couple of hours at the vise.

And if I sat by his elbow quietly and waited long enough, he'd eventually pat his lap and invite me to climb up. I'm sure I was the only kid in my elementary school who could roll a wood-duck wing and wind a hackle feather and make a whip-finish.

My flies never looked like Dad's, as carefully as I tried. The bucktail on my streamers tended to flare out at odd angles, the heads came out too big and lumpy, and the wings of my dry flies never seemed to cock quite right. I refused to tie a standard pattern. Everything that came from my vise was an invention. But when I finished my fly for the evening I'd take it from the vise and hand it to Dad, and he'd hold it up and squint at it, and then he'd hand it back to me and nod and say, "Yup. This one'll catch fish, all right."

Through the months of the fly-tying season my own little box of flies would slowly fill, and when the fishing season arrived I'd try them and discover that Dad was right. As flawed and amateurish and outlandishly colored as my creations were, they *would* catch fish.

Fly-Tying Season

I gradually figured out that *anything* would catch fish if you tied it onto your leader and kept it in the water long enough. Nevertheless, I always took it as a compliment when Dad said, "It'll catch fish." And since those winter evenings on my father's lap, I have never really wanted to catch fish with anybody else's flies.

In my family the seasons turned regularly and predictably. My father followed the demands of the season as if he had no choice, and the rest of us adapted because Dad gave us no choice.

The annual telephone call from old Charley Watkins, who owned the cabins on Sebago Lake, officially heralded spring. After he hung up, Dad would give us his imitation of Charley, who spoke loudly to compensate for his own deafness. *"The wind cracked her open, Mr. Tapply,"* Dad would scream. *"Ice went out today. You boys better get on up here, you hear?"* Charley's phone call from Maine triggered a series of phone calls by Dad, the landlocked salmon Paul Revere of eastern Massachusetts, and by Friday afternoon he'd mustered the salmon crew—Dad, Gorham Cross, Dick and Put Putnam, Tom Craven, and sometimes Tap's boy. We crammed ourselves into a station wagon and went churning up the Maine Turnpike for a weekend of trolling and casting Nine-Twelves and Gray Ghosts and Supervisors into the frigid April winds around Doctor's Island and Kettle Cove. We only managed a few trips a year, because the spring sun quickly warmed the surface water and the smelt stopped swarming around the mouth of the Songo River and *Salmo sebago* soon sank down out of fly-rod range.

The salmon season dovetailed neatly into the trout season—late April through mid-June. The trout season actually was comprised of several subseasons—Quill Gordon, Hendrickson, and Light Cahill. By the middle of June the mayflies stopped hatching on the Squannacook and the Ipswich, and the warm surface waters on Walden and the Cape ponds drove the fish to the bottom.

The warming of the waters, however, enticed the large-mouths into the shallows, marking the beginning of the bass season. For two months of summer evenings we paddled the shorelines of the Charles and Sudbury rivers, coming the weed beds and the sunken trees and the dark holes under overhanging brush with deer-hair bugs.

I wouldn't say Dad ever grew tired of fishing, but by late August he would begin to seem distracted, and one evening after supper, when the air was cool and some of the swamp maples were showing crimson, he'd pile me and Duke the setter into the car and we'd go looking for pheasants. Ringnecks were bountiful in our parts back then, and we had only to wait until the chicks were fully fledged and able to fly to work the dog on them. We hunted them like quail—except without guns. Duke would zigzag through the shoulder-high fields—too fast and too wide at first, so Dad had to scream and blast on his whistle and stomp on the check cord. In August, after nine months of no bird smells in his nostrils, Duke usually bumped the first brood or two. They would rise up from the fields covey-like, six or eight of them, brown birds, because the yearling cocks didn't have their colors yet, and Dad and I would mark them as they scattered. Then we'd chase down the singles, and by the end of the first evening Duke usually had remembered how to point.

If we fished in September, it was a Saturday afternoon of bluegilling with dry flies, and it seemed out of season. We were counting the days until the upland season opened in New Hampshire.

Beginning the first Saturday after October 1, every weekend found us lugging our twenty-gauge doubles through New Hampshire thickets and trying to keep up with Duke. We hunted with Burt Spiller on Saturdays, prowling his Tripwire and Schoolhouse and Mankiller covers around Rochester and Gilmanton Iron Works and Alton. Burt strictly observed the Sabbath, so he put aside his shotgun on Sunday. Dad and I observed it differently, so after the woods got too dark to hunt on Saturday we dropped off Burt and drove to the Valley Hotel. And on Sundays we chased grouse and woodcock around Hillsborough and Hennicker and East Washington.

The bird season ended for us abruptly on November 15, the day the New Hampshire deer season opened. Grouse were still legal, but Dad figured the woods belonged to the men with rifles and red hats.

From Thanksgiving to Christmas Dad hunted ducks and deer and I stayed home. Opening day of the next significant season in my family came on January 1, when Dad set up his fly-tying desk in the living room.

I don't observe the seasons as rigidly now as Dad did when I was growing up. I usually manage to fish for trout at least once in every month of the year, and I've often sandwiched midge fishing for trout and bugging for largemouths around a day of woodcock shooting in October. And I tie flies year-round.

Dad always seemed to know what flies he'd need for the upcoming seasons—or else he limited himself to fishing with the flies he had, I don't know which. He tied a year's supply when the season was open for fly tying, and when it closed he packed his stuff away. I don't recall ever seeing him tie out of season.

My approach is different. Before a June trip to the Green I make two dozen cicada imitations in anticipation of that unique "hatch." I tie Hendricksons on April evenings and Pale Morning Duns during the weeks before our Montana trek in August. Generally when I return from a day on the river I ponder the flies I wish I'd had, and I sit down and tie some of them, even though I know I'll probably need something else the next day.

Last summer Andy and I set up the vise in the car where we were parked on the banks of the South Fork of the Madison, and we spent the afternoon tying caddisflies in anticipation of the hatch that never materialized.

We tied midges on the Delta flight that was taking us to the Frying Pan in Colorado (a foolproof way to strike up conversations with blond flight attendants), and we've scattered wisps of marabou and elk hair and olive dubbing on motel-room carpets all over Montana.

We've huddled in the cabin beside DePuy's Spring Creek trying to make imitations of the sulphur emergers that the trout were sipping outside the window.

I always need to be ready to respond to the impulse to make something. Fly tying solves problems, but it's also my therapy. I find that my mind keeps turning to a new way to tie wings on a midge or to make black beetles visible to my middle-aged eyes. So I keep my fly-tying desk set up year-round, and I visit it when the creative spirit moves me.

I know that I can get by with just a few proven patterns. That doesn't stop me from experimenting. I've spun wool heads onto Gartside soft-hackle streamers and added bead-chain eyes. I don't know if Jack does that or not. I've tried weaving bodies of contrasting chenilles onto my Woolly Buggers. I've created an endless variety of emerger patterns, using every kind of fur and feather in my desk. My current obsession is to fashion a simple crab imitation that will sink properly and actually fool a permit. I've tried chenille, rug yarn, and spun wool so far. Some of them sink beautifully in my bathtub, but I have yet to consult a Belize permit.

Just this morning (it's January as I write, threatening snow, temperature in the low twenties—high fly-tying season) Cliff Hauptman called to regale me with tales of "jiggering" through the ice for yellow perch. He described the jig he uses—a little teardrop spinnerblade with soldering and a plastic bead dangling from the bend of a gold hook. He was very specific about the design of the successful jiggerbait. Nothing else, he averred with typical certainty, works.

Cliff's a good fly fisherman. But he's a pragmatist. If something else will work better than flies, that's what he uses. Not me. I want to prove that nothing works better than flies. So after we hung up, I sat down and made some jiggering flies. Wraps of lead, spun Globug yarn at the bend, Flashabou, and Poly Flash. Damn, it looks good! Cliff and I are going to have a contest.

Of course, if I should outfish him, he will insist that what I made isn't a fly, and he'll prove it by pointing out that every ingredient in my concoction is synthetic.

We'll argue about it. Neither of us will back down.

I've tied an incredible amount of junk, although I'm sure all of it will catch fish.

Sometimes I've actually solved problems at my vise. One

March evening, while my legs were still thawing after a fishless afternoon of standing in thirty-nine-degree water, I spun wisps of deer hair onto #24 hooks that fooled midging Swift River rainbows the next day. Another time my frustrated imagination produced tiny nymphlike floaters with stubby laid-back wings and sparse closely clipped hackles that Nelson's Spring Creek trout seemed actually to prefer over natural emerging sulphurs. Whimsy has prompted me to combine odd colors of marabou and bucktail and deer hair and bead chain into Bastard Buggers. Bass and brown trout eat them.

Last fall I shot pheasants, woodcock, ruffed grouse, quail, and chukar. I saved all their feathers, and I've been trying to imagine uses for all of them. I've been known to screech to a halt beside what my kids call road pizzas and take my Buck knife to the bloody carcasses of raccoons and squirrels and woodchucks and possums. I've found some interesting applications for Christmas tree tinsel, chamois cloth, and old felt hats.

A couple of years ago I invented the Canine series of flies (the Pup Pupa, the Hair-of-the-Dog Emerger, the Cairn Caddis, among others). The primary ingredient was the belly hair from Duncan Barnes's Cairn Terrier. Duncan has not yet reported on the effectiveness of the Canine series.

Dad tied Dark Tigers and bass bugs and his own mongrel dry fly, the Nearenuf. And that was about it. He fished with just a few patterns in a variety of sizes and never seemed to feel handicapped. By the time Charley Watkins made his annual telephone call from South Casco, Maine, in April, the fly-tying stuff had been packed away in mothballs, and we didn't see it again until the following New Year's Day.

Although I tie year-round, I still honor the fly-tying season the way Dad did. January through March is the time for restocking the depleted fly boxes. That's when I make a year's supply of my own standbys, just as he did, and, like Dad, I need to be prepared to share them with my friends.

If the fly-tying season opened and closed by government edict, and if I were restricted to tying my flies only from January through March, I could get through a trout season with just nine patterns. They're all easy and fast to tie and require no exotic materials, complicated techniques, or specialized tools.

Here's what I tie by the scores during the long winter months when fishing opportunities are rare and it's open season at the fly-tying bench:

PHEASANT TAIL NYMPHS. I make them the way Craig Matthews and John Juracek do, with peacock herl for the thorax. In sizes fourteen through twenty, they serve just about any nymphing occasion. They accurately imitate dozens of mayfly nymphs. Weighted, they are deadly bumped along the bottom. Unweighted, they drift or can be twitched in the film to fool trout keyed on emergers.

MIDGE PUPAE. A few winds of Krystal Flash, Flashabou, or gold wire around the shank of a #20, #22, or #24 nymph hook, with a couple of turns of peacock or ostrich herl at the head, makes the fly that solves most of my problems for midging trout. And I can tie a year's supply in one evening.

GRIFFITH'S GNATS. Easy to make and a universal midge imitation. Since trout feed on midges year-round, I always carry a good supply with me. I simply palmer a few turns of grizzly hackle over a peacock-herl body. Trout eat larger (#14 and #16) Griffith's Gnats when they're feeding on clumping midges. I find the small ones (#22 and #24) work when the fish are "smutting" on individual midges.

BEETLES. I now make them with black foam, which I've found to be superior to deer hair. They float forever, are more durable, make a better shape, and are easier and quicker to tie. A few winds of grizzly hackle around the neck, clipped flush with the bottom, makes legs. I leave a hackle collar sticking up around the neck for visibility. I've found that summer trout will fall for beetles just about any time—even when they are feeding selectively on a mayfly or midge hatch.

RUSTY SPINNERS. These will take most trout that are sipping spinners, regardless of the species of mayfly. I believe trout key on the silhouette and the translucent wings, not the body color. I tie mine with divided-hackle-fiber tails, quill abdomens, rust-colored dubbed thoraxes, and sparse sparkle-yarn wings.

COMPARADUNS. They seem to fool the most selective risers, whether they are keying on emergers, cripples, or duns. I use a few wisps of brown sparkle yarn for the tail (which presumably represents the trailing nymphal shuck). I tie some with gray, some with yellow, some with olive, and some with orange bodies (which, in a variety of sizes, seem to match all of the hatches I usually encounter), and I've found that a few turns of grizzly or dun hackle trimmed flush with the bottom works as well as flared-hair wings and is easier to tie.

SOFT HACKLES. This simple little bug meets four situations: caddis pupa, drowning caddisflies, emerging mayflies, and crippled mayflies. It can be fished dead-drifted in the film or sunken and twitched toward the surface. Although it can be tied in many colors, I make most of mine with a few turns of peacock herl (there it is again, peacock herl—great stuff—I use it for everything) for the body, one wind of partridge breast feather (one wind only—sparseness is the key to the soft hackle), and another couple turns of peacock herl at the head.

ELK HAIR CADDIS. I just tie in a bunch of hair behind the eye so that it flares tentlike over the shank of the hook, and then I clip the front to a little head. It's got the right profile and floats low on the water but can still be twitched and skittered without sinking. Size matters more than color. Dubbed or peacock-herl bodies with clipped palmered hackle are optional. I generally don't bother with bodies.

WOOLLY BUGGERS. In various colors and sizes, the dependable Bugger is the only streamer I need. Bluegills, crappie, trout, bass, pickerel, bluefish, and stripers eat them. I intend to discover if bonefish and tarpon will, too. I make them sparse and thick, drab and brilliant, large and small, and in every imaginable combination of colors. On some I spin deer-hair or wool heads, add bead-chain eyes up front, and a few strands of Flashabou to the tail. When

I'm tying Woolly Buggers, my creative juices flow. Buggers can imitate baitfish, leeches, crawfish, or just about anything else that swims. Small pink ones look like shrimp. They can be dragonfly larvae or stonefly nymphs. It's the magic of marabou.

About the time Sarah turned nine, she began to drag a chair up beside me when I was working at my vise. She'd sit there, her chin propped up on her fists, with her wide brown eyes watching my hands. Of course, I eventually patted my lap, and, of course, she clambered up onto it.

With my hands guiding her fingers, we tied a Woolly Bugger together.

"Now you make one by yourself," I said.

She selected the brightest colors I had on the desk— white marabou, yellow chenille, red hackle. I reminded her to keep tension on the thread, but otherwise I kept my mouth shut. Her little fingers fumbled awkwardly with the half-hitches. The head came out kind of lumpy and the tail was too short. But she did it herself.

When she finished, she took her creation out of the vise and handed it to me. Her arched eyebrows asked my opinion.

I held it up, squinted at it, and nodded. "It'll catch fish," I pronounced.

Months later she trolled her own Woolly Bugger behind the boat on Great Pond in Maine, and a smallmouth bass ate it. Mike and Melissa and I cast and trolled a variety of the sleek things I had tied, but Sarah's was the only fish of the day.

❦ *9* ❦

Throwin' Streamers

THE BOW RIVER DRAINS THE ROCKY MOUNTAINS IN
western Alberta and flows southeasterly directly through
the center of Calgary, the province's largest and most modern city. Northwest of Calgary—that is, upstream—the
Bow runs glacier-cold and relatively sterile, and does not
offer dependable trout fishing. Once the river enters the
city limits it begins to pick up interesting nutrients that
might cause one to hesitate before eating a fish that grew
up there, but that nourish the growth of weeds and insects
and other creatures and organisms that cause trout to grow
fat. East—downstream—of Calgary, the Bow abruptly
leaves the train yards and skyscrapers of the city behind.
Here it winds through unspoiled forests and rolling plains
and rock-strewn canyons. Eagles and ospreys cruise the
river course. Lone herons and rafts of pelicans pluck fish
from the waters. Deer and bear tramp the mud banks.
Rainbow and brown trout abound in these waters. Big ones.

The Bow has earned its reputation as one of North America's premier trout rivers. When Andy and I floated it several Memorial Day weekends ago, we landed, among dozens in the fourteen- to eighteen-inch range, six trout of more than twenty inches. Well, Andy landed most of them.

Frigid rain accompanied us during the three days we fished the Bow that May. We wore high-tech long johns under our neoprenes, woolen caps folded down over our ears, insulated vests under our rain gear, and gloves. When the sun set, slush formed in the guides of our fly rods.

Hell, it was Canada. And the fishing was good.

We caught our trout by dredging weighted nymphs through deep runs and chucking Woolly Buggers against the banks. We had hoped for some dry-fly fishing.

But one of Andy's browns measured twenty-three inches. It ate a streamer that could only have come from Andy's vise, a mongrel he calls The Fly That Ate Montana. Our guide, Peter Chenier, told Andy exactly where to cast for that fish.

When Andy and I returned to the Bow it was October. Alberta generally basks in Indian summer weather in early October, Peter had told us. I talked to him on the telephone several times in September. No frost yet, he kept saying. The river was low and clear, the air warm and dry. Wonderful hopper fishing. Blue-Winged Olives on cloudy days.

Elliot Schildkrout and Ralph Freiden and Randy Paulsen came with us. Elliot and Randy are psychiatrists like Andy. Ralph's a physician.

I'm a history teacher.

Our plane touched down in Calgary around midnight. The landing was tricky. A fall blizzard was sweeping across the Alberta plains and blanketing the city.

"I feel bad for Randy," Andy confided in me as we rode the taxi from the airport. "After all, he's never been fishing before. We've told him all our stories, the joys of fly fishing for big trout. He's invested in all that brand-new equipment. He was going to go to fly-casting school, but it got cancelled. Now he's gotta fish in the snow."

The cable weather channel in our hotel room was not encouraging. Snow, temperatures around zero (that was Celsius, we finally figured out, to our relative relief), winds from the west. Big winds, forty gusting to seventy. That, too, was by some metric scale that we couldn't translate, but which we presumed meant something less than miles per hour. It still sounded bad.

The forecast proved accurate. In the morning the river-banks were white and the skies sooty. Fine grains of snow blew almost horizontally down the river. Peter took Andy and me to the section of the river within the city limits where, on nice days, businessmen in suits cast dry flies to rising trout during their lunch hours. "The browns are moving upstream with sex on their minds," Peter told us. "This isn't the most scenic float, unless you're into bridge abutments and grain elevators. But it's where we should find some big ones."

No dry-fly fishing today. We rigged our 7-weights with sink-tip lines and tandems of weighted Woolly Buggers. White on the dropper, black on the point, was Peter's prescription. Today we would throw streamers.

With Andy in the bow seat and me in the stern, we probed the banks and channels. It was not delicate fishing. Weighted streamers land with a significant plop, which is proper. That plop signals nearby trout that a meal has arrived. The fish charge from their lairs behind boulders, in eddies, against logs. Throw, strip, lift, throw. Cover the water. False-cast and you miss a potential lie.

Andy and I make an uncommonly good team at throwing streamers from a driftboat. We try to land our flies inches from potential trout hidey-holes. We know how to mend quickly upstream so that our Buggers are not swept away from fish-holding pockets by the faster midriver currents. We make several casts a minute. We waste no energy. From the bow seat, Andy casts at a downstream angle. He hits the soft buffer directly ahead of a boulder; I hit the eddy behind it. He throws into the pocket below the bush whose branches sweep the surface of the water; I sidearm a tight loop under the bush.

It's not that different from the fly-rod bass-bugging that obsesses us back home. Except on a big trout river like the Bow the current keeps us moving, and the targets whiz past no matter how hard the guide rows upstream, and a mis-cast or hesitation means a potential crocodile brown trout missed.

We have figured that we average three casts a minute apiece, each cast averaging fifty feet. Between us in an hour we cast well over three miles of fly line, barring time-outs for playing fish.

We cover the water.

For the first couple of hours that first wintery October morning, we covered all the water. We had a bump here, a tug there, a swirl, a follow. They were hitting short. We hooked no fish.

Randy, the rookie, was floating the same stretch of river as we were. He was fishing alone so he could have the full attention of his guide. We floated past him in the middle of the morning. He had gone ashore. He held up two gloved fingers. A V for victory. A question. Any luck?

We shook our heads. No, we hadn't caught anything either.

He yelled, waving his V sign. Over the rush of the river and the city noises around us, we heard him. "Two. I got two."

Andy and I grinned at him and pumped our fists. We held our hands up, palms facing each other. How big? He showed us. Fourteen or fifteen inches, it looked like. Andy and I exchanged smiles. We were happy for him, we assured each other.

We floated on. Peter held the boat in an eddy below a highway bridge so we could throw into the steaming outflow below the sewage treatment plant. We detected a faint sulphur odor on the snowswept wind. A bright green weed bed grew against the current line. Trucks rumbled overhead. "A hot spot," proclaimed Peter.

A moment later Andy grunted. His rod bowed. Fish on. Before he landed it, my Bugger stopped hard. Doubles. Mine measured nineteen inches, Andy's an inch shorter. I caught another. Andy lost one. This was more like it.

We met up with Randy and his guide again in the middle of the afternoon. We beached our boat beside theirs to stretch our muscles and compare notes. By now Andy and I had each taken another trout, fat sixteen-inchers. We were feeling fine.

Randy told us diffidently that he had caught two more browns. Bob Lowe, his guide, said he'd measured them. One was twenty-one inches. The other twenty-two.

Randy was smiling, but it was hard to know what he was

thinking after his first day of trout fishing. I suspected he simply figured this is how it worked. Get a streamer into the water and eventually four trout will eat it. They'll be rather large and they'll pull hard. It's cold, but fun, though the scenery isn't what you see on calendars.

One twenty-one inch trout makes a good year for me.

It was still snowing the next day. The wind had abated. The air was colder. Andy and I floated a scenic stretch of river east of the city where steep piney banks fell to the water and boulders and logjams and beaver houses provided a continual series of targets for our casts. Today we were grim for the tasks. We had catching up to do. The rookie was showing us all up. We were happy for him, proud of him. Yesterday Elliot and Ralph had caught very few fish. Now it was time for the veterans to show their stuff.

We raked the banks all morning without a strike.

After lunch, Andy and I dredged some channels with nymphs and managed to land a few respectable rainbows. The largest measured eighteen inches.

By late afternoon ice began to clog our guides. Our reels kept freezing solid. We threw streamers some more. It was a way to keep our blood circulating. We had no strikes.

Elliot and Ralph reported very slow fishing. Each caught a couple on stonefly nymphs. One was seventeen inches.

Randy stuck to the streamer. He caught only one fish all day.

It was a brown. Bob measured it. It was twenty-five inches long.

On our third and last day on the Bow the five of us managed, among us, to land four fish. Three were ten-inchers. Andy got one that stretched out to sixteen.

On the third day Randy got skunked.

Somewhere in this tale there lies a lesson. A rank novice, a man who had never fished before, who could barely, by dint of repeated false-casting, slop a Woolly Bugger thirty feet from the boat, this—this *neophyte*—outfished four experienced trout fishermen for three days on a world-class trout river.

Why?

The due reward of a very nice man, a kind of poetic justice?

The Red Gods? I have always believed in them. Sometimes I have, after my fashion, prayed to them.

The law of averages? I always believed in it, too.

Irony? It exists in nature as well as literature.

Maybe one, or some combination, of those unknowable forces. Or maybe it was just the luck factor that is inherent in all streamer fishing from a driftboat, the democracy of the trout river that does not discriminate between expert and novice. When fishing this way, you expect to make many casts for every strike. You have to hit every target, but you know that a trout doesn't lurk in every likely looking place. You just don't know which spots are inhabited, and of those that are, you don't know which ones are inhabited by the big ones. You have to hit them all.

Randy caught the three largest fish of the trip. He happened to hit three places where big trout lived. Luck, okay, perhaps. Or perhaps his guide, knowing Randy couldn't cover all the water, and knowing his river, made sure that Randy hit the best places. Or maybe Randy stripped more slowly than the rest of us, or retrieved closer to the boat before lifting to cast again. Maybe he fumbled inexpertly with his line, allowing his Woolly Bugger to sink deeper before he began his strip. Maybe his short casts took his fly through lies farther out from the banks than where Andy and Elliot and Ralph and I, showing off our casting skills, fished. Maybe he was using a longer and finer—or shorter and stubbier—leader than the rest of us.

I'm a fisherman. I'm not supposed to believe in luck. I must believe in skill and knowledge and experience. I believe in explanations. I just don't know what the explanation for this is.

Streamer fishing is a leveler. That's the lesson. There really is an element of chance (all right, call it luck) that is significantly absent from fishing with dry flies or nymphs, where drag-free presentations, a delicate and practiced hand, and precise hatch-matching almost always separate the skilled angler from the rookie and neutralize the luck factor. Streamer fishing demands less finesse. A streamer in the water, whether it's dragged, twitched, stripped, jigged, or dead-drifted, can catch a trout. Sometimes a large trout.

When Andy and I floated the Beaverhead last summer, we flung streamers against the willows that lined the banks. We used identical flies, we probed the pockets with identical intensity and accuracy, we retrieved with identical one-foot strips. And I outfished Andy four to one.

A week later, during an afternoon's downpour on the Missouri, Andy turned the tables on me with a vengeance. It made no sense.

In a way, the randomness of it is consoling. If you know you're doing the right thing, you can shrug and wait for the Red Gods to turn their smiles upon you, or the law of averages to catch up, or whatever it is.

When Andy and I throw streamers from either end of a

driftboat, we find a rhythm that quickly becomes mesmer-
izing. When we're doing it right, we function as a team. I
lift my line from the water as Andy's cast settles upon it.
With one eye I note where Andy's fly has landed. Mine will
fall at the next target downstream. As my fly hits, Andy lifts
to cast. Over and over we repeat, and miles of riverbank
melt away behind us. It's never boring. For every cast there
is a target. Every target may hold a fish. We never know.
We've done it enough, deposited enough memories into the
bank, to keep our attention from wandering no matter how
many hours pass without a strike.

When the trout haven't gathered into pods to eat tiny
mayflies off the surface, or when they're not concentrated
in channels sucking nymphs off the bottom, streamer-
throwing is usually the best way to catch them. Or at least
it's the best way to catch big ones. Streamers are a trout
mouthful, worth chasing. And especially under the right
water conditions—when the river is rising, perhaps a bit
discolored by a recent or current storm—big trout like to
move into the softer currents against the banks. They look
for cushions where they can rest while awaiting worthwhile
delicacies to float past—in front of or behind rocks, beyond
foamy current lines, in eddies and backwaters, under overhanging brush.

There are other ways to fish streamers. They can be
trolled or cast in ponds from a canoe or float tube. A wade
fisherman can cover all the water in a small stream with a
little Woolly Bugger or leech. I caught a twenty-one-inch
rainbow from the Box Canyon by dead-drifting a six-inch
strip of rabbit fur around a boulder. Bob Lamm suckered a
big brown trout from a pool in Red Rock Creek by jigging
a black-and-yellow marabou streamer up and down on the

bottom, a technique I scoffed at until Barry Beck did the same thing, with the same result, in a little Pennsylvania spring creek.

The fly rodder's standard method for catching ice-out landlocked salmon from Maine's Sebago and Moosehead lakes and Winnipesaukee in New Hampshire is to troll streamers that imitate smelt, the salmon's staple forage, while the bow man casts against the rock-strewn shorelines. In theory, the salmon will follow the cast streamer and, if he doesn't hit it, will then strike at one of those being dragged behind the boat. This rarely happens unless the wind is blowing onshore, the water temperature is right, and the stars and planets are properly aligned, three conditions that sometimes actually coincide, usually when I'm not there. I've spent a lot of cold fishless days in a boat while salmon fishing. But the memory of hooking just a few of those silver leapers keeps me going back.

There's romance in the names of traditional Maine salmon streamers—Warden's Worry, Supervisor, Nine-Three, Mickey Finn, Professor, Chief Needabah, Edson Dark Tiger and Edson Light Tiger, Gray and Green and Black Ghost. Each has its precise recipe. Even the ingredients are exotic—jungle cock, golden and silver pheasant, peacock herl, badger and squirrel hair, bucktail, teal and goose and wood duck and hackle feathers, tinsel and floss and chenille. Tied with careful attention to prescribed pattern, they are gorgeous creations—works of art, really. I suppose some traditionalists still use them.

I have a box that holds a collection of those old streamers. They were tied by my father forty years ago. They're classics, like old Leonard fly rods and Parker twenty-gauges. I take them out and look at them now and then.

But I haven't tied one on in years—not to protect my collection, for I'd use one of them without hesitation if I thought it would be the most effective fish-fooler. So much for my reverence for art.

Nowadays my functional streamer collection consists almost exclusively of Woolly Buggers and Gartside soft-hackles in every possible combination of color and size, weighted and unweighted. The main ingredient in both designs is marabou. I make them to imitate smelt, baby trout, shiners, and leeches, on the theory—which I doubt—that such imitation makes a difference. They're simple and fast to tie. They take trout and salmon, largemouths and smallmouths, pickerel and pike, bluefish and stripers.

On the Bow River in October, Randy Paulsen used a simple black Woolly Bugger. So did the rest of us.

Randy caught the three biggest fish of the trip.

Go figure.

10

The Extra Terrestrials

AS A TEENAGED DRY-FLY FANATIC IN THE 1950s, MY problems were simple and my successes abundant. I tied on a #14 Nearenuf or spent-winged Adams and caught plenty of surface-feeding trout in New England. The fish seemed to be conditioned to mayflies, and whether or not an active hatch was apparent, I knew what would work: light tippets, drag-free floats, and something that more or less suggested a mayfly.

My heart still swells when I see trout sipping mayflies. I travel thousands of miles and invest a lot of money so I can cast self-tied Pale Morning Duns and Blue-Winged Olives onto western rivers where big browns and rainbows eat the real things. I always consider it time and money well spent, regardless of how successfully I manage to match the hatch and catch the trout.

If my local trout rivers experienced reliable mayfly hatches, I might be content to confine my fishing to New

England. Sadly, however, for most of my streams most of the time, the mere sight of a lone cream-colored mayfly drifting through a current causes me to pause, smile nostalgically, and consider the day a success.

Oh, the Hendricksons still hatch on the Farmington in April, barring high and muddy water, and I witnessed a Quill Gordon hatch on a little brook a mile from my house last May, a cause for celebration even though it failed to bring trout to the surface. But by mid-May the Farmington browns feed almost exclusively on midges, because that's about all there is for them. And I have *never* seen a trout eat a mayfly on the Swift. The Squannacook appears sterile. Ditto the Nissitissit.

Although I know that there still remain a few clean fertile streams in the East where mayflies thrive and trout live on them, I believe I have seen the future of trout fishing. The same forces that have destroyed self-propagating trout populations in many of my rivers—deforestation, acid rain, various kinds of pollution, and general neglect—have extinguished the fragile mayflies. Trout can be stocked. Mayflies can't.

I'm still a dry-fly nut. And I still fish New England trout rivers. But I have learned to tie on an imitation beetle or ant when I want to prospect for rising trout. No longer are my trout conditioned to eat mayflies. They eke out a meager living on other things, as often as not stuff that's virtually invisible to the human eye. Sometimes I find fish gobbling midges that, were I to try to imitate them, would have to be tied on hooks smaller than a printed question mark.

But trout will eat terrestrials. They eat them in the middle of a midge glut. They eat them when they are feeding opportunistically. They eat them in preference to the odd mayfly that floats over them. They eat them when no terrestrials appear on the water. They eat them when they otherwise appear to be eating nothing whatsoever.

Terrestrials are, by definition, land-based insects whose presence on water is accidental. The health of terrestrial species is independent of the health of trout rivers and streams. Terrestrials, therefore, provide a stable food source for even our most sterile trout waters.

In recent years, terrestrial imitations have become my standby trout flies.

I haven't figured it all out yet. Sometimes my trout spurn my beetle imitations but accept my ants. Sometimes it's the other way around. When neither gets results, a little analysis leads me to try fake crickets or grasshoppers or green inchworms. Rare is the day when I can't catch some fish on a terrestrial imitation.

Rare is the day when, minus a significant hatch, I *can* catch a trout on a mayfly imitation.

Mayflies still thrive in western rivers, and western trout still gorge on them. But even on fertile waters as diverse as the Henry's Fork, the Madison, the Bighorn, and the Paradise Valley spring creeks, trout actually seem to prefer terrestrials. Frequently when frustrated by complex mayfly hatches, I have fooled fish easily with a terrestrial. When no trout are rising, I *know* I can catch some on ants or beetles. My fly of choice during midge hatches is a big beetle.

Sometimes terrestrial-eating trout can be quite selective, and the fisherman must match the "hatch." When hoppers are blowing onto the water, only a hopper imitation of the right size and color will work, and the fish will completely ignore all other patterns, terrestrial or mayfly. I've had the same experience during a fall of flying ants. Similarly, I have found that inchworm imitations only work when I find these little larvae dangling from their filaments in stream-side bushes. But at these times, *only* inchworms will do. When the trout will only take small red ants or large green-ish beetles, as they sometimes will, closely examining what's floating on the water gives the fisherman a convinc-ing explanation.

Usually, however, trout appetites for terrestrials seem random and indiscriminate, and usually my fly selection is equally whimsical. Various species of ants, beetles, and crickets are ubiquitous, and I tie on a generic imitation of one or the other. Trout will generally eat whatever terres-trial tidbit drifts near them regardless of what kinds of real bugs are actually on the water.

Terrestrials are the future of dry-fly fishing.

Utah's Green River boasts, by some accounts, the densest population of large trout in the lower forty-eight. In June every one of those fish is easy pickin's. They lie every-where—against the banks, along current lines, in big ed-dying pools—with their noses pointing toward the surface. They smash with unrestrained belligerence every inch-long black-and-white fly that floats near them. Andy and I boated and released an estimated 120 trout on a one-day Green River float last June. Several were in the twenty-one to twenty-two-inch range. Fifteen-inchers disappointed us.

The fishing, in fact, was too fast, too easy, and one day of it satiated us. We spent the rest of our trip looking for greater challenges.

We were lured to the Green by guide Mike Howard's

tales of a fabulous hatch. Not green drakes, not salmonflies. Not Tricos or *Hexagenia* or PMDs.

Not mayflies or caddis or stoneflies. Not aquatic insects at all.

Cicadas.

Cicadas?

The American periodical cicada, which we know as the seventeen-year cicada, is a terrestrial insect. It lives all but a few weeks of its life as a larva underground. Then it crawls up, hatches, lives briefly as a winged bug, lays its eggs, and dies.

If all cicadas underwent metamorphosis according to the same period, they would appear only once every seventeen years and would have no significance whatsoever for trout or trout fishermen.

I have read that cicadas are considered trout food in New Zealand. Otherwise, I have been able to find no reference to them in angling literature.

The Green River cicada hatch has not yet achieved the mythic reputation of some of the other fabulous hatches that lure line-tangling hordes of fishermen to storied trout rivers. But, inevitably, it will. And inevitably, perhaps, it will be discovered that other trout in other rivers are equally greedy for cicadas.

Vincent C. Marinaro, in his classic *A Modern Dry-Fly Code*, introducing his chapter on the Japanese beetle, wrote, "What a rare thing it is to witness the advent of an entirely new insect on trout waters."

The man who, only a few years ago, fashioned an imitation cicada and cast it upon the Green River, must have felt as Marinaro and his friend, Charles Fox, did back in the early 1940s when they first tried beetles on Pennsylvania's Letort Spring Run. That Utah angler learned that his Green River trout were absolute suckers for cicadas, and suckers as well for even relatively crude cicada imitations.

In June, the trees that border the upper section of the Green buzz with the mating songs of male cicadas. These big bugs are cumbersome flyers, and when they try their wings, they don't get far. Some of them fall or are blown onto the water where, presumably, thousands of trout lie in wait for what must be a delectable bellyful.

And yet during that entire day that Andy and I caught trout continuously on our fake cicadas, we didn't see more than half a dozen real cicadas actually floating on the water, nor did we spot *any* fish actually feeding on them. Mike Howard told us that Green River trout begin to smash cicada imitations within a few days of the first buzz in the streamside woods and continue to be duped by them well into July, long after the time that adult cicadas complete the final brief stage of their lives. Yet, according to Mike, it's unusual to find trout feeding with any regularity on the real things. "There really aren't that many cicadas actually on the water," says Mike. "They sure do love these fakes, though."

Green River trout, in other words, crash anglers' outlandish cicada flies with unrestrained zeal *despite the fact that relatively few real cicadas are available for them to eat.*

These are facts worth pondering. They parallel my experiences with other terrestrial fishing on other trout waters. They suggest theories that might help to explain the hunger trout have for terrestrials, why terrestrial imitations work so well under a variety of conditions, and why some patterns work better than others. These theories are probably unprovable, since they require us to make assumptions about the psychology of eating behavior in trout—but that's what we fishermen do all the time.

Theory 1: Terrestrials are so delicious that trout prefer them to other more abundant food, and this becomes imprinted in what passes for a trout's brain. Anglers have long surmised, for example, that the formic acid flavor of ants is irresistibly tasty to trout, which will eat them, when available, in preference to mayflies.

Theory 2: One large terrestrial, such as a cicada, hopper, or cricket, is a meal all by itself. Survival-tuned trout learn that they can consume a bellyful of nutrition on a single meaty terrestrial while exerting a fraction of the energy it would require for a comparable meal of mayflies. If the food value of a few big terrestrials equals that of dozens of tiny mayflies, perhaps the mere presence of half a dozen hoppers on the water sparks the same kind of "selective" feeding response in a trout as does a full-blown pale morning dun hatch.

Theory 3: Because terrestrials are delicious and/or an economical meal, certain terrestrials need to be available only occasionally to create a conditioned response in the trout, impelling them to fall for imitations even when none of the real things is actually present on the water. Other trout on other rivers, never seeing or tasting these bugs, do not respond to their imitations. Trout don't have to eat many ants, beetles, or whatever terrestrial insects fall into their water to become conditioned to accepting them *whenever they appear*—or whenever a reasonable facsimile floats nearby. Something that looks more or less like an ant, for example, will seduce any trout that has munched ants, regardless of whatever else may be available to him. For the same reason that nonimitative mayfly patterns used to fool trout, so do generalized ant patterns work.

Theory 4: If any of the preceding theories is true, it follows that it takes very few actual bugs on the water to focus the attention of trout and cause them to feed on terrestrials selectively. A terrestrial "hatch" needn't be lavish to turn on the fish. On the other hand, when terrestrials fall into the water, they float low in the film or sink beneath the surface and are not readily observed by fishermen, so perhaps terrestrials are really far more abundant in the water than we believe.

Theory 5: A corollary to Theory 3, this theory holds that as more fishermen attempt to catch trout with fake terrestrials, the fish will grow increasingly wary of the imitations. Generic terrestrial patterns will lose their effectiveness. More and more, we will have to find precise sizes, colors, and designs to fool trout. This, it seems to me, is what has happened with mayfly hatch-matching.

Using terrestrials requires the same skills as does any other dry-fly fishing. You still have to find and stalk your trout, and you still have to cast accurately. Realistic presentations—slender tippets and drag-free floats—are still mandatory. Trout react aggressively to a hopper, beetle, or cricket imitation that hits with a soft "plop," probably because naturals that fall or are blown onto the water land that way. Because natural terrestrial insects are not at home in the water, they float low or sink, so imitations must mimic this trait. Any hackles on fake terrestrials should be trimmed flush with the bottom to prevent them from riding too high.

The Extra Terrestrials

Ant and beetle imitations, which are small and dark and should float half-submerged in the surface film, are devilishly hard for the angler to see on the water. I like to tie in a collar of grizzly hackle at the neck of my beetles, and I make my ants with little flashy tinsel wings, for the sake of visibility. The trout don't seem to object.

I still love the challenge of trying to match a mayfly hatch. But increasingly, my experiences on trout rivers East and West have convinced me that imitating land-borne insects gives me my best chance to catch trout consistently.

I always carry extra terrestrials with me.

11

A Gift Trout

A CERTAIN MARCH DAY COMES TO NEW ENGLAND
every year when the sun shines brighter and warmer than
it has for six months. It's the best day of the year. I believe I
can taste that sunshine. I want to lap it off my arms. I close
my eyes and lift my face to it and open my mouth to drink.
On that one day the sun unlocks the water that has been
frozen all winter. The snowbanks melt so fast that I can see
them shrink. The snowmelt runs downhill, following the
contours it finds in the hard earth. It gathers volume as it
goes, creating rivulets that cut streambeds alongside the
roadways, miniature but complete trout streams with well-
defined pools, runs, flats, and riffles. The earth itself begins
to thaw, and I am intoxicated on the primal organic smell
of decay and rebirth that the sun releases from the ground
on that March day. That's when I first notice that the alders
are greening and the maples are reddening. In the swamps
the pussy willows burst into fuzzy blossom.

The sap begins to flow on that certain day in March—not only in the trees, but in the trout fisherman. I feel rivers coursing through my veins. I must go fishing.

For the first half of my life I could not answer this urge. April 15 was Opening Day in Massachusetts. So when that first magical spring day arrived in March—*my* opening day—I had to content myself with prowling the boggy swamps and walking the banks of swelling streams. I carried a stick, not a fly rod, and with it I poked at mounds of soggy leaves to uncover the pale little snouts of new skunk cabbage and ferns. I tossed twigs into the streams and watched them bounce on the currents, imagining the mayflies that would follow them in a month or two.

Then came the year when they changed the law. No open season, no closed season. Fish whenever you like, said the new law, which was kind of a cruel joke for us Massachusetts trout fishermen. Hatchery trucks populate our trout streams in the spring. They cannot make their deliveries until the thaw, which begins on that bewitching March day, has ended, and the dirt roadways dry up and become passable.

Nevertheless, I carried a fly rod with me on that first legal March opening day many years ago, and I stuck a little plastic box of dry flies into my pocket. I did not expect to make a cast. But I could still go fishing.

In those days I fished for trout in just two ways: worms and dry flies. In both cases I used a fly rod. I chose my method according to my mood, and I generally caught hatchery trout either way. Stockers would rise to a floating fly in the riffles and pockets whether or not bugs were on the water; conversely, rising trout would eat a worm drifted unweighted near them.

I had never caught a trout on a spent-winged spinner or emerger or nymph. I had never even tried.

The stream that beckoned me that day empties a large swamp. Then it funnels through a boulder-strewn crease between two hills before it flattens in a meadow, narrows again to meander through woodland, and finally empties into a pond. In the pockets among the boulders, against the undercut banks, in the riffles and pools, the hatchery trout take up residence during the season and eat caddis and mayflies, not to mention the worms and dry flies I cast there.

The snowmelt had just started on that March day. The stream still flowed at its winter level, low and clear. Ice shelves bordered its shaded banks, and while patches of bare earth showed in the sunny places, blankets of dirty snow still huddled under the low boughs of streamside evergreens.

I walked downstream for a mile or more, happy enough to be carrying a rod and to have the sun warming the back of my neck, to hear the stream gurgle and to flush an occasional early robin and to smell the earth and the water.

I did not expect to see a trout, and when I did I believed—as I still believe—that he was the only trout in the entire stream that day. He was feeding steadily in a quickening of the current where it narrowed between two boulders. He was, I knew, a pioneer, a brave adventurer, a genetic one-of-a-kind. He had had the singular sense to avoid eating cheese-flavored marshmallows and salmon eggs the previous spring. He had somehow inherited enough instinct to flee the stream where he had been dumped before it killed him. He had found summer sanctuary in a spring hole in the pond, survived the winter, and then, perhaps only a few days earlier, had swum two miles upstream to this place where the stream narrowed into a food funnel.

He wasn't a native trout, of course. He had been born in a hatchery. There were no native trout in this stream. But he was a carryover trout, a laboratory freak born, against all the odds, with a unique combination of recessive genes that gave him both the will and the wiles to be a survivor. He was as close as we generally come in eastern Massachusetts to a wild trout. He was, therefore, a special trout. A miracle.

He was exactly what I had come seeking and had not dared hope to find.

This trout was a gift to me on this special March day. And he was rising regularly—to what I couldn't tell. There were no bugs on the water.

I tied on a dry fly. Pattern or size did not concern me. It had never mattered much. I flicked it back and forth, happy to be casting again. One good drift, I knew, would catch this trout.

Except it didn't. He ignored my fly. He continued to feed. I could see him suspended there in the current. With clock-like regularity he would lift in the water so that his dorsal protruded above it, and his head would twist to one side or the other. Then he would sink back under the surface. I put the fly over him half a dozen times, trying to time it to his feeding rhythm. Once he ate something barely an inch from my fly.

Wrong fly, then. Good, I thought. Thank you. Hatchery trout had always been easy. I would have been disappointed had this gift trout been easy. I tried something else— smaller or larger, lighter or darker, I don't remember. Another dry fly. I had no science for it then. It didn't matter. I could not raise him.

A worm would have done him in, probably. Trout always ate worms. That had been my experience.

But I didn't regret having no worms with me. It was better this way. This way it had to be a puzzle, a challenge, and it seemed to fit the spirit I found myself in on that perfect afternoon.

I stripped in my line and sat on a rock to watch my trout. Finding him feeding in my stream on this March day was a gift, and I was thankful for it. It should have been enough, I thought, just to have him there.

I usually tipped my cap and walked away from the trout that refused my fly. I had done it plenty of times. It never bothered me. There were always others, and I never tried to analyze too closely why I couldn't catch any particular one. I always believed that if I caught every fish I tried for it wouldn't be much fun and left it at that. I also believed that if I *really* tried for every hatchery stocker I found, I *would* catch it.

But this trout, I decided, I really wanted to catch. He was a worthy opponent. Figuring out how to catch him on a fly would make this special day perfect.

I was, I know now, a naive, ignorant fisherman in those days. I knew virtually nothing of aquatic entomology. I had observed, but never studied for the purpose of understanding, the behavior of trout. But on that March day many years ago, I tried to study my gift trout. He was no more than twenty feet from where I sat. I could clearly see the crimson and bluish spots on his copper sides, and I could measure him. He was a brown trout and he was at least fifteen inches long, larger than any trout deposited by a Massachusetts hatchery truck. And after a while I noticed something peculiar: When he rose to feed, his back broke the surface of the water, but his head remained submerged. He ate with a quick sideways dart of his mouth and then sank back. He was rising. But what he was eating did not float. It had to be drifting an inch or so beneath the surface, where my trout's mouth winked.

I knew that mayflies live as larvae on the streambed, then float up to the surface where they metamorphose into winged insects. I had read that trout feed on all stages of the mayfly's life cycle. But I had only fished with dry flies, and I usually caught my share of trout. None of the rest of it seemed important. All discussions of precise imitation, of nymphs and emergers and crippled duns and spinners, had struck me as arrant nonsense, simply the affectation of writers intent on making things more complicated and eso- teric than they really were.

But this trout, although he must have seen my dry fly float over him, seemed to insist that his food come to him an inch under water. It was a revelation.

Dry-fly fishing is an exercise in plane geometry. Every- thing takes place on two dimensions: the length and width of the surface of the stream. The trick is to place the fly upstream of a feeding trout so that it will float directly over him in the same manner as a natural insect. The plane— the surface of a stream—carries several different currents moving at different speeds, and the skilled dry-fly fisher- man can read those currents. He will manipulate his line and leader across that plane surface so that it will not pull on the floating fly, causing it to drag in an unnatural manner. That is the challenge of dry-fly fishing.

The nymph fisherman contends with three dimensions. His is an exercise in solid geometry. Drag-free drifts are as important in nymphing as they are in dry-fly fishing. It's not enough to drift a sunken fly along the particular current line where the target trout lies. He must also drift it at the proper depth. And while he still must manipulate his line across varying surface currents, he must also account for the third dimension—the fact that currents near the surface travel at different speeds from those closer to the bottom.

Nymph fishing is the most challenging and difficult of all forms of fly fishing. Not only must the angler make a drag-free presentation that neutralizes vertical as well as horizontal currents, but he must also tie on the proper imitation and present it at the precise depth where the fish are feeding. And he cannot always see those fish. Sometimes they feed right off the bottom, sometimes they are suspended somewhere between the bottom and the surface, and sometimes they are feeding just beneath the surface.

On the other hand, the most unskilled of fly-fishing novices, anglers who cannot cast twenty feet of line and who have no understanding whatsoever of river currents or trout behavior or aquatic entomology, catch large trout on nymphs. Guides on the Bighorn and Green and Madison rivers sit their beginners up in the bows of their driftboats. They tie on a Pheasant Tail or stonefly nymph, add a split shot, and fix a neon-pink cork strike indicator to the place where the leader joins the line. "Just hang it over the side and let it drift along with the speed of the boat," they tell their clients. "When the pink thing goes under lift the rod." It's still-fishing with a bobber from a moving boat. Anybody can do it.

But climb out of that boat, wander away from that guide, and everything changes. Now the fisherman must seine the water or turn over rocks in order to guess what the trout might want to eat. Mayfly or stonefly nymph? Caddis or midge larva or pupa? Scud or cranefly? And what size and color? He must read the complex current speeds himself. He must analyze the water to figure out where the fish are lying and at what depth. He must adjust the amount of lead he pinches onto his leader and the length of leader between the fly and the strike indicator. Or, if he wants to do it properly, he eliminates the strike indicator and relies on a combination of Zenlike feel and an unwavering focus on the place where the line dips into the water to identify the trout's delicate take. He must lob his fly to the place that will allow the current to bring it to the fish, and he must mend his line to prevent drag. He must follow the drift of his invisible fly with his rod tip, holding his arm high to minimize the amount of line on the water.

Nymphing is exhausting, both physically and mentally. It's tedious. It's difficult.

It's deadly.

All of the really large trout I've caught have been taken on nymphs. There were several monster rainbows from Colorado's Frying Pan River—one of them clanked Andy's DeLiar down to its eight-pound limit. He might have weighed nine or ten. He was lying in six feet of water when he ate my weighted #16 shrimp pattern. The tip of my fly line barely hesitated when he mouthed that fly.

And there was the brown trout that Barry Beck spotted for me on Fishing Creek one rainy September morning. He was a shadow on the bottom of a flat run and we couldn't tell how big he was. I stalked him from behind and cast a nondescript gray nymph upstream to him. Barry directed me. "No, a foot to the left and two feet upstream. . . . He should've seen that one. . . . Wait, he's moved. . . . Okay, two feet to the right, now. . . . Yeah, good. . . . He's moving . . . he sees it . . . there!" That brown measured a half-inch under two feet.

There have been others on the Bow and the Bighorn and the Box Canyon. I am convinced that the most and the biggest trout are caught by skilled nymph fishermen.

All the successful dry-fly fishermen that I know are expert casters. Their skills are observable and easy to admire. They are artists, and what they do is beautiful. They can drop a fly into a teacup at forty or fifty feet. They throw right and left curves and puddle casts in any fickle wind. They can read currents and they can mend line.

The best nymph fishermen I know seem to have mystical powers. They work their magic beneath the visible surface—metaphorically as well as literally. I've watched Dave Schuller maneuver nymphs through riffles and dropoffs on the Bighorn, but as carefully as I watch him, I find little to imitate. His casting technique is—well, it's primitive and efficient, but it isn't beautiful. It's nothing like the way he casts a dry fly. The fly rod is not designed to throw lead weight. There's no false casting, no artful loops arcing over the water and settling gracefully on its surface. Dave lobs, mends, drifts, lifts, lobs again. It looks repetitive and boring. I can do it, more or less. There's not much pleasure in lobbing nymphs the way there is in casting a dry fly.

Skillful casting is the essence of dry-fly success. For the nymph fisherman, an accurate cast is a minor mechanical step in what otherwise seems to me to be a complex intuitive process. The skill lies in what precedes the cast and what follows it. Dave has tried to teach me the nympher's craft—how to read the water to figure out where a large trout lies; how to decide where to cast and how to judge the currents and manipulate the entire length of line and leader so that the nymph will arrive at that large trout free-drifting at the proper depth; how to sense the delicate and momentary take, and how to distinguish it from the fly or the weight ticking the bottom; how to adjust the leader length and the amount of lead twist-on; and how to have both the patience and the intensity to make these adjustments constantly, depending on the continually changing character of the water.

I'm still not very good at it. For me, dredging nymphs is something to do while waiting for trout to rise. With this attitude, I suppose I'll never master the craft.

Sight-fishing with nymphs, on the other hand, replicates the dry-fly angler's art. When trout are eating nymphs in shallow runs or riffles, or when they lie suspended just beneath the surface, it's a visual game. The nymph needn't be heavily weighted, so I can cast it like a dry fly. I can watch the fish, see him take. This is my kind of nymph fishing. It's how I started.

I sat on that sun-warmed boulder and watched my gift brown trout on that March afternoon half a lifetime ago, and I figured it out. I opened my fly box. It was full of dry flies.

But wait. On the bottom of one compartment, hidden

beneath a White-Winged Wulff, I found a drab little brown thing without hackles. I had plucked it from a streamside bush a year earlier. I knew what it was called. It was a Pheasant Tail Nymph.

I tied it on and tossed it six feet upstream of my trout. I couldn't see the fly, so I watched the fish. When he lifted toward the surface and winked his mouth, I raised my rod. I felt the throb of his life in my fingers, and then I saw my gift trout dart toward the bottom. A moment later he leaped. He seemed to hang there suspended against the yellowing streamside willows, his flanks reflecting the warm gold of that March sun.

And after I landed him and unhooked him and released him, I sat again on that boulder and thought about it. It was quite wonderful. I had discovered nymph fishing. I felt that. I had discovered it all by myself.

That discovery, not the trout himself, was the gift of that March day. No. That discovery was the gift the trout had given to me.

I bit off that Pheasant Tail Nymph and made a separate compartment in my fly box for it. Then I unstrung my rod. I trudged back upstream, looking for new skunk cabbage under the wet leaves and flushing robins and savoring the sunshine.